HOMEMADE MIXES FOR INSTANT MEALS—
THE NATURAL WAY

Books by Nina and Michael Shandler

THE MARRIAGE AND FAMILY BOOK
YOGA FOR PREGNANCY AND BIRTH
WAYS OF BEING TOGETHER
HOW TO MAKE ALL THE "MEAT" YOU EAT FROM WHEAT

Homemade
Mixes
for
Instant Meals—
The Natural Way

Nina and Michael Shandler

RAWSON, WADE PUBLISHERS, INC.
New York

Library of Congress Cataloging in Publication Data

Shandler, Nina.
   Homemade mixes for instant meals—the natural way.

   Includes index.
      1. Cookery (Natural foods)   2. Convenience foods.
I. Shandler, Michael, joint author.   II. Title.
TX741.S53   1981   641.5′637   80-51253
ISBN   0-89256-145-9
ISBN   0-89256-150-5   (pbk.)

Published simultaneously in Canada by McClelland and Stewart, Ltd.
Composition by American—Stratford Graphic Services, Inc.,
Brattleboro, Vermont
Manufactured in the United States of America by R. R. Donnelley &
Sons Co., Harrisonburg, Virginia

Designed by Jacques Chazaud

First Edition

Contents

CHAPTER ONE

A Menu of Mixes   3
    Natural Homemade Mixes   4
    Setting Up   9
    Making Mixes   11
    Using Mixes   11
    Variety from a Single Mix   12
    Refilling the Empties   12

CHAPTER TWO

Breakfast Mixes   13
    Basic Buckwheat Pancake Mix   14
    Basic Corn Wheat Griddle Cake Mix   17
    Basic Rice Griddle Cake Mix   19
    Basic Raisin Coconut Oatmeal Mix   23
    Basic Malted Cracked Wheat Cereal Mix   26
    Basic Spiced Millet Porridge Mix   28
    Bran Flakes   30
    Variety Flake Granola   31
    Sesame Buckwheat Granola   31
    Coconut Raisin Granola   32

Malted Wheat Cakes 32
Molasses, Wheat Germ, Raisins and Nut Cereal 33
Sweet Wheat Puffs 33

CHAPTER THREE
Light Soup and Gravy Mixes 35
Basic Cream of Onion Soup Mix 36
Basic Clear Onion Soup Mix 38
Basic Cream of Mushroom Soup Mix 41
Basic Light Brown Mushroom Soup Mix 43
Basic ABC Soup Mix 45
Basic Japanese Seaweed Soup Mix 47
Basic Herb Broth Mix 50
Basic Dark Broth Mix 52
Basic Nut and Raisin Soup Mix 55

CHAPTER FOUR
Salad Dressings and Dip Mixes 58
Basic Parmesan Cheese Mix 59
Basic French Dressing Mix 61
Basic Herb Dressing Mix 65
Basic Italian Garlic Dressing Mix 67
Basic Spicy Mexican Dressing or Sauce Mix 70
Basic Curried Dressing Mix 72

CHAPTER FIVE
Hearty Bean Mixes for Stews, Casseroles and
Main Dishes 75
Basic Southern Black-Eyed Pea Mix 76
Basic Boston Bean Mix 80
Basic Dark Variety Bean Mix 84
Basic Split Green Pea Mix 87
Basic Curried Chick-Pea Mix 91
Basic Middle East Style Chick-Pea Mix 95
Basic European Lentil Mix 99

Basic Kidney Bean Mix 102
Basic Mexican Pinto Bean Mix 109

CHAPTER SIX
Rice and Other Grain Mixes 114
Basic Indian Rice Pilaf Mix 115
Basic Middle Eastern Rice Pilaf Mix 119
Basic Spanish Rice Mix 121
Basic Middle Eastern Bulgur Mix 123
Basic Spiced Kasha Mix 125
Basic Herb 'n Onion Millet Mix 128

CHAPTER SEVEN
Yeast and Quick Bread Mixes 131
Basic All Purpose Whole Wheat Bread Mix 132
Basic Rye Bread Mix 147
Basic Oatmeal Wheat Bread Mix 152
Basic Quick Whole Wheat Bread or Muffin Mix 155
Basic Bran Muffin Mix 164
Basic Cornbread Mix 167

CHAPTER EIGHT
Cake and Cookie Mixes 170
Basic Cake Mix 171
Basic Ginger and Spice Cake Mix 180
Basic Carob Cake Mix 187
Basic Cookie Mix 192
Basic Oatmeal Cookie Mix 197
Basic Spice Cookie Mix 200

CHAPTER NINE
Pie, Pudding and Frozen Dessert Mixes 205
Basic Whole Wheat Pie Crust Mix 205
Basic Coconut Crumble or Crust Mix 208
Basic Wheat Germ Crumble Mix 210

Basic Carob Pudding Mix   211
Basic Pudding Mix   215
Basic Mincemeat Mix   220
Basic Dried Fruit Compote Mix   223
Basic Sweet and Nutty Rice Dessert Mix   226

GLOSSARY   231
INDEX   233

HOMEMADE MIXES FOR INSTANT MEALS—
THE NATURAL WAY

CHAPTER ONE

A Menu of Mixes

The day just isn't long enough. When we add up how many hours we need just to live our routine workaday lives, it usually comes out to about twenty-eight. And, judging by the pace of people around us, many are in the same predicament; perpetually trying to make up those elusive four or more hours. Since the earth is uncompromising about its speed of rotation and simply refuses to slow down, the problem of inventing time-saving devices has been relegated to human ingenuity.

Convenience fast foods are one such solution that we all know very well. In this day and age when inflation dictates our life-styles and working for our daily bread often leaves no time to bake it—or cook much else—convenience foods would seem to be a lifesaver. However, nutritional experts raise some questions in this regard. The Senate Select Committee on Human Needs and Nutrition reports: "The simple fact is that our diets have changed radically within the last fifty years, with great and often very harmful effects on our health." Another government survey conducted recently is expected to show that less than half of the nation is receiving adequate nutrition.

Poor and rich alike live, on the average, with a diet that is 45 percent fat, 24 percent sugar. The remaining 31 percent of the average diet contains chemical additives.

With more than half the population now existing on such inferior fare, it should be no surprise that medical costs rose from $27 billion a year in 1960 to $137 billion in 1976. Although inflation accounts for some of this, the bulk of this huge cost increase was spent on cancer, arteriosclerosis and diabetes. All three of these killer diseases have now conclusively been linked to diet.

We are faced with a serious dilemma. The demands on most of our lives require constant driving activity. We simply don't have the time to cook wholesome, health-giving meals three times a day. Yet the fast foods we have come to depend on are not providing our bodies with adequate nutrition.

Natural Homemade Mixes: Convenient, Inexpensive Food Value

With this dilemma in mind, we have compiled this cookbook. It provides a convenient, easy and economical way to maintain a busy life-style and to be nutritionally responsible at the same time. This book presents more than fifty basic mixes that can be prepared in large quantities, stored and then cooked with the simple addition of liquid ingredients. These basic mixes can provide hundreds of different meals. Each basic mix can be made into several different dishes merely by varying the liquids and the amount of liquid added to the basic mix. Thus, a sweet rice mix can be cooked with milk to make rice pudding, or with tomato juice to get sweet-and-sour rice or with water for a side dish of sweet grain. The recipes are wide-ranging, including soup, legume, grain, dressing, bread, muffin, cake, cookie and dessert mixes. All of these mixes are completely natural: free of sugar, chemical additives, refined grains and flours. By using these mixes with fresh fruits, vegetables and dairy products, a total and highly nutritious diet can be created.

In one afternoon—the time it takes to prepare a festive meal—two months of mixes for breakfast foods, lunches, dinner dishes and snacks can be mixed, bottled and labeled.

When the jars are on the shelves the major work of daily cooking is eliminated. There is no need to plan; the entire menu is at your fingertips. Just choose a mix or two for each meal, add liquid, cook and serve. With the great variety afforded by each and every basic mix, meals and treats can be interesting, with healthy homemade goodness, while preparation and planning time can be cut to a manageable minimum for the modern and often harried cook.

Let's Compare: Commercial Mixes Versus Natural Homemade Mixes

If there is any doubt about the value of spending a few hours preparing your own mixes, a nutritional comparison of commercial dried soup mixes and homemade dry soup mixes will conclusively allay your suspicions. The commercial dried soup mixes have recently, as a result of saturation advertising, become the mealtime rage.

Have you noticed that these instant soup mix companies often don't bother to list the nutritional data on the package? If they did, the list would indeed be brief. A serving of the most popular dried noodle soup would boast 7 percent of the Recommended Daily Allowance (RDA) of thiamine, but would only give .4 percent to 3.9 percent of other nutrients. All of the other dried soup mixes are equally poverty-stricken from a nutritional point of view. As for protein, the vast majority of dried soups contain under 4 grams while one brand of pea soup has a higher protein content—5.4 grams. The majority thus provide less than 9 percent of a woman's RDA while the pea soup provides less than 12 percent.

Compare the meager percentages of commercial mixes with the nutrition provided by homemade mixes:

Commercial Dried Green Pea Soup—
  Percentage of RDA
Protein—12%   Thiamine (B_1)—7%
            Other Nutrients—Less than 4%

Homemade Curried Split Pea Soup Mix—
Percentage of RDA

Protein—26%	Thiamine (B_1)—37%
Iron—19%	Riboflavin (B_2)—12½%
Phosphorus—18%	Niacin—12%

Other Nutrients—Less than 12%

This comparison of pea soups shows that you get more than twice the nutritive value from a homemade mix—*and at less than half the cost of the commercial kind.*
A comparison of the nutritional content of a homemade noodle mix and the most popular brand of noodle soup is even more convincing.

Commercial Chicken Noodle Dry Soup—
Percentage of RDA

Protein—9%	Thiamine—7%

All Other Nutrients—Less than 4%

Homemade Noodle Mix Cooked in Tomato Juice—
Percentage of RDA

Protein—35½%	Iron—28%
Calcium—21%	Magnesium—12%
Vitamin A—54%	Pyridoxine (B_6)—21%
Thiamine (B_1)—100%	Folic Acid—100%
Riboflavin (B_2)—60%	Niacin—17%

Other Nutrients—Less than 12%

If you choose to cook your homemade noodle soup mix with milk the percentages change substantially, but all remain high, especially when compared with their commercial counterpart.
Nutritionists generally agree that each of our three meals should provide nearly a third of our Daily Recommended Allowance of protein, vitamins and minerals. Obviously, a homemade mix contributes greatly to accomplishing this.

Chemical Additives and Flavorings
in Commercial Mixes

Salt is responsible for most of the flavor of commercial instant soups and lunch dishes. An average dried soup contains .9 grams of salt per serving. Our bodies need between .02 and .06 grams of salt *per day.* A cup of dried soup can easily give us fifteen times our daily requirement of salt.

Since too much salt can lead not only to high blood pressure but also to kidney problems, heart and blood vessel conditions and skin disorders, the wisdom of taking such a salt overdose is highly dubious.

Monosodium glutamate (MSG) is another ingredient used in virtually every dried soup, lunch dish, gravy and salad dressing mix in the supermarket. A dried soup may contain as much as ¼ teaspoon of MSG per serving. This popular chemical often produces dizziness, facial pressure and a burning sensation throughout the body in large numbers of people and also produces severe brain damage in experimental animals.

Although it may be that some preservatives and chemical additives are safe for human consumption, the uncertainty of many has led the Senate Select Committee on Human Needs and Nutrition to report: "The varying degrees of testing, the quality of testing, and the continuing discoveries of apparent connections between certain additives and cancer . . . give justifiable cause to seek to reduce additive consumption to the greatest degree possible."

Too Much Sugar

Of all the additives in convenience foods, sugar is by far the most excessively used. Sugar is hidden in almost every prepackaged food in astonishing quantities. Wyler's Beef Bouillon is nearly 15 percent sugar; Hamburger Helper is 23 percent sugar; Barbecue Shake and Bake is 50.9 percent sugar. And for the products that are obviously sweet, Jell-O's cherry-flavored mix is 82.6 percent sugar while a prepackaged Sara Lee cake will give you a mere 35.9 percent sugar, substantially less than Barbecue Shake and Bake.

Sugar intake can lead directly to tooth decay, hypoglycemia, diabetes, obesity and arteriosclerosis. In addition it inhibits the natural desire for highly nutritional foods and can deplete the body of valuable B vitamins—phosphorus and potassium—thereby contributing indirectly to additional health problems such as anemia and susceptibility to colds and infections.

Dry presweetened breakfast cereals are without a doubt the most grievous offenders; they often contain more than 50 percent sugar.

Refined Carbohydrates Compared with Unrefined Carbohydrates

Even after sugar is subtracted from a packaged cereal, the remainder is, by and large, refined and enriched carbohydrate. The most commen refined enriched carbohydrate on the grocery store shelves is enriched wheat flour. This substance is a major ingredient in nearly every packaged mix that can be bought, including not only cereals but soups, cakes, cookies, breads, pies, macaroni and noodles.

Enriched white flour is white flour with vitamins added to partially replace the vitamins that are deleted from whole wheat when refining it into a white powder. In making mixes at home we do not recommend using refined enriched white flour, but always advise the use of whole grain flours and whole grain pastas. The reason is simple and straightforward. Whole grain products contain a higher quantity and quality of essential nutrients than refined grain products.

A Cost Comparison

Beyond the questionable nutritional value of "convenience" foods, there is the exorbitant cost of these products to consider. Homemade mixes are one way to cut food costs suddenly and dramatically. By making our own mixes, grocery bills can be reduced 30 percent to 50 percent.

And in making our own mixes we begin to pay for food rather than for extravagant multimedia advertising and high profile packaging.

In the end, it is the consumers, you and I, who pay the costs of advertising and fancy packaging. But we don't have to. We can still save a lot of time and cut our cost of living by making our own convenient mixes. And, in the long term, we will be healthier as well as wealthier.

Homemade mixes can be the basis for your entire day's menus—breakfast, lunch, dinner and snacks—or they can be an invaluable addition that you resort to at times when a nutritious meal is needed in a hurry. Begin your mix-making by looking over this book, then list the mixes you would like to stock. Once you have done that you are ready to set up your kitchen for processing.

Setting Up

To start mix-making you may need to make some simple additions to your kitchen crockery, minor readjustments to your cabinet space and your grocery shopping.

Jars and Bottles

You need wide-mouth bottles or jars for storing mixes. All mix recipes suggest the appropriate bottles for that mix. These vary from 8-ounce jars to half-gallon jars. If you have a collection of mayonnaise, mustard and pickle jars these are perfect for storing your mixes. If, however, you have thrown away or recycled your jars, the quickest way to accumulate inexpensive airtight containers is to buy a supply of canning jars in appropriate sizes.

Labels

Each jar needs to be labeled to differentiate one mix from another. Any sticky-back label large enough for you to write the name of the mix on and the page number where it can be found in this book (giving the right proportion of liquid required, variations and serving suggestions) will do.

Storage Space

Depending on the number of mixes you intend to use you may need to clear some space in your cabinet before beginning.

All the mixes in this cookbook are made from dry ingredients and do not require refrigeration. However, flours lose nutritional value when stored for longer than two months at room temperature. If you are expecting to keep a mix containing flour for a longer period of time it would be wise to plan to store it in the refrigerator or another cold place.

Grocery Shopping

Shopping for mix ingredients may involve buying larger quantities of basic supplies less often than is your usual habit. It may also require greater use of a well-stocked natural food store and fewer visits to the supermarket.

Begin to create your shopping list with the names of the mixes you intend to make in hand. Next, turn to the pages where the mix recipes are located. Write down each ingredient needed and the amount required.

This grocery list of specific ingredients in needed quantities will enable you to avoid overbuying as well as overspending. If you follow your list carefully you will not fill your cabinets with "basic" supplies that will never be used, thus saving space and money.

Making Mixes

Mixes can be made in one of two ways. Either set aside a morning, afternoon or evening to make a large number of mixes, or make them as you need them. No matter which way suits you, the technique for making mixes is simple and uniform. Dry ingredients are combined, placed in jars, labeled and stored. Ingredients in mixes should be thoroughly combined to ensure even distribution of flavors. Jars need to be sealed tightly before storing to ensure freshness.

Every basic mix in this cookbook is made in a suitable quantity to feed you and your family several times without having to mix up a batch of new dry ingredients. Most mixes are stored in wide-mouth jars and serving size amounts are measured out every time you make pancakes, soups or baked goods. Beans and grain dishes, however, are stored in several small one-cup or 12-ounce bottles. Each bottle is used to serve four persons at one meal. This variation in storage method is to ensure that each dish made from the mix contains a proper amount of seasonings for the best possible flavor. As with any recipes, mixes can be halved or doubled to meet your particular needs.

Using Mixes

In using mixes care should be taken to create a balanced and nutritious diet. Homemade breakfast mixes include pancakes and hot and cold cereals. These are all made with whole grains and a minimum of sweetening in the form of barley malt or blackstrap molasses. However, the addition of some high quality protein food such as milk or eggs and fruit is needed to make a totally well-rounded first meal.

A balanced homemade mix lunch might include a serving of convenient quick soup mix, a salad with a mix dressing and a serving of cheese on a homemade mix muffin. Dinner meals should include both grain and bean mixes in order to give a complete protein. Fresh vegetables should be added to any main meal and these can be made more interesting if topped with a mix dressing or sauce or served with a mix dip.

In addition to balanced mix-based meals, nutritious mix snacks can be made available with little fuss or bother. Hot cookies, muffins and cakes can be prepared in a few minutes.

Variety from a Single Mix

Each homemade mix can make *several different dishes simply by changing the liquid ingredients* added to the dry mix. For example, Split Green Pea Mix can be served as Hearty Green Pea Soup, Green Pea and Rice Stew, Green Pea and Millet Casserole, or Green Pea and Vegetable Soup. French Dressing Mix can be made into French Dressing, French Fruit Dressing, Cream Cheese French Dressing, Sour Cream French Dressing, Avocado Dressing, Beet Dressing, Blue Cheese Dressing or Horseradish Dressing. The result is great diversity in meals with no more time in the kitchen!

Refilling the Empties

Favorite mixes never need relabeling. You simply clean and refill the bottle. Other mixes that are not staples in your diet can be relabeled and filled with another mix to keep your menu and meals changing.

Homemade mixes are a simple way to rediscover wholesome good meals without sacrificing precious hours of your time to the kitchen.

CHAPTER TWO

Breakfast Mixes

The convenient breakfast foods in this chapter include pancake mixes and hot and cold cereal mixes. All are made from whole grains to give maximum fiber and natural nutrition to the first meal of the day.

A large variety of pancakes are given. Each mix can be made with eggs and milk, buttermilk, apple juice or soy milk. Fresh berries can be added as a special morning treat. For fancy pancakes, sliced fruit can be topped with whipped cream, or applesauce can be topped with sour cream. With mixes all prepared pancakes can be served in a hurry even on mornings when the whole family needs to leave early for school or work.

However, if your schedule allows not even a moment for standing over a grill waiting for pancakes to bubble, some pancake mixes double as breakfast bars, cookies or muffins. These variations can be baked in the morning for a hot morning treat or in the evening for a quick breakfast food.

Hot cereal doesn't have to mean soggy oatmeal. Hot cereals can be tempting as well as wholesome if you use a variety of grains such as rice, millet, cracked wheat, oatmeal, wheat flakes and rye flakes mixed with dried fruit or spices. Cooked in milk rather than water these cereals become smooth and creamy high-protein foods. With fresh fruit added they become a good rival for old-fashioned grain pudding. If hot cereal is left over, mold it in a loaf pan. Then slice, dip in egg and fry to provide a nutritious "French toast."

Granola is not the only healthy cold cereal alternative you can stock. Periodically everyone needs a breakfast in a box or a bag. If granola is becoming a bore, or if you never liked it in the first place, try making your own version of Nutty Shredded Wheat Nibbles, Malted Wheat Smacks, Bran Flakes, and storing them in half-gallon jars.

The only sweeteners used in these cold cereals are barley malt and blackstrap molasses. Barley malt is made from sprouted barley that is then cooked until it forms a thick, sticky, nutritious sweet syrup high in B vitamins and enzymes. It is a concentrated whole grain which is not damaged in cooking, as is honey. Blackstrap molasses is the residue of sugar cane that remains when all the white sugar is removed, and contains the major nutritional value of the cane. It is an excellent source of iron. One tablespoon supplies one-third of the adult minimum daily requirement of iron. In addition it contains more potassium than any other food, and is rich in B vitamins copper, magnesium, phosphorus, pantothenic acid, inositol and vitamin E. Just one tablespoon contains over 100 milligrams of calcium, or approximately one-third the calcium in 8 ounces of milk. For these reasons we believe these two sweeteners are the only ones good enough to add to the preparation of a healthy basic breakfast food.

BASIC BUCKWHEAT PANCAKE MIX
(Makes 2 quarts mix)

2½ cups whole wheat pastry flour
5¼ cups buckwheat flour

1 teaspoon salt (optional)
7 teaspoons non-alum baking powder

In a large bowl, combine all ingredients and mix thoroughly. Place in a half-gallon wide-mouth jar, seal tightly and store in cool dry cupboard. Use within two months.

BUCKWHEAT PANCAKES (*Serves 4*)

Preparation and Cooking Time: 20 minutes

1 egg   1 cup milk
1½ cups Buckwheat Pancake Mix

In a bowl, beat together egg and milk. Stir in mix until combined. Heat a lightly oiled griddle or heavy frying pan to medium hot. Drop batter onto griddle using a serving spoon or ladle. When pancake surfaces are covered with bubbles, flip over and cook until lightly browned on the second side. Serve with butter and syrup or malt.

BUTTERMILK BUCKWHEAT PANCAKES (*Serves 4*)

Preparation and Cooking Time: 20 minutes

1 egg   1½ cups buttermilk
1½ cups Buckwheat Pancake Mix

In a bowl, beat together egg and buttermilk. Gradually stir in mix until well combined. Heat a lightly oiled griddle or frying pan to medium hot. Drop batter onto griddle using a serving spoon or ladle. When pancake surfaces are covered with bubbles, flip over and cook until lightly browned on the other side. Serve with butter and syrup or malt.

APPLE BUCKWHEAT PANCAKES (*Serves 4*)

Preparation and Cooking Time: 20 minutes

3 eggs
1 cup apple juice
1 cup Buckwheat Pancake Mix

In a bowl, beat eggs until lemon in color. Beat in apple juice. Stir in mix until combined. Heat a lightly oiled griddle or heavy frying pan to medium hot. Drop batter onto griddle using a serving spoon or ladle. When the pancake surfaces are covered with bubbles, flip over and cook until lightly browned on the other side. Serve with syrup, malt or applesauce.

APPLESAUCE AND SOUR CREAM BUCKWHEAT CAKES (*Serves 4*)

Preparation and Cooking Time: 25 minutes

1 egg
1 cup milk
1½ cups Buckwheat Pancake Mix

1 cup unsweetened applesauce
1 cup sour cream

In a bowl, beat together egg and milk. Stir in mix until combined. Heat a lightly oiled griddle or heavy frying pan to medium hot. Drop batter onto griddle using a medium-size spoon or ladle, to make 12 pancakes. When pancake surfaces are covered with bubbles, flip over and lightly brown the other side.

Spread each buckwheat cake with a layer of applesauce and a layer of sour cream. Stack in threes and serve with an extra dab of applesauce on top.

BUCKWHEAT BLUEBERRY PANCAKES (*Serves 4*)

Preparation and Cooking Time: 20 minutes

1 egg   1½ cups Buckwheat Pancake
1 cup milk   Mix
               ⅔ cup fresh blueberries

In a bowl, beat together egg and milk. Stir in mix until combined. Fold in blueberries gently. Heat a lightly oiled griddle or heavy frying pan to medium hot. Drop batter onto griddle using a serving spoon or ladle. When the pancake surfaces are covered with bubbles, flip over and brown lightly on the other side. Serve with butter and syrup or malt.

BASIC CORN WHEAT GRIDDLE CAKE MIX
(*Makes 2 quarts mix*)

4½ cups cornmeal   1 teaspoon salt (optional)
3¼ cups whole wheat pastry   2 tablespoons non-alum
   flour   baking powder

In a large bowl, combine all ingredients and mix thoroughly. Place in a half-gallon wide-mouth jar, seal tightly and store in cool dry cupboard. Use within two months.

CORN WHEAT GRIDDLE CAKES (*Serves 4*)

Preparation and Cooking Time: 20 minutes

1 egg   1½ cups Corn Wheat Griddle
1 cup milk   Cake Mix
1 tablespoon oil

In a bowl, beat egg, milk and oil until well combined. Stir in mix until a smooth batter forms. Heat a lightly oiled griddle or frying pan to medium hot. Drop batter on griddle using a serving spoon or ladle. When the griddle cake surfaces are covered with bubbles, flip over and lightly brown the other side. Serve with syrup or malt and butter.

BUTTERMILK CORN GRIDDLE CAKES *(Serves 4)*

Preparation and Cooking Time: 20 minutes

1 egg   1½ cups buttermilk
            2 cups Corn Wheat Griddle Cake Mix

In a bowl, beat together egg and buttermilk. Stir in mix until combined. Heat a lightly oiled griddle or frying pan to medium hot. Drop batter onto griddle using a serving spoon or ladle. When the griddle cake surfaces are covered with bubbles, flip over and lightly brown on the other side. Serve with butter and syrup or malt.

CORN COTTAGE CHEESE GRIDDLE CAKES *(Serves 4)*

Preparation and Cooking Time: 20 minutes

2 cups cottage cheese   ⅔ cup Corn Wheat Griddle
4 eggs   Cake Mix

In a bowl, mix cottage cheese and eggs until combined. Stir in mix to form a batter. Heat a lightly oiled griddle or frying pan to medium hot. Drop batter onto griddle using a serving spoon or ladle. Brown griddle cakes on both sides until done. Serve with applesauce or malt.

CORN PEANUT BUTTER GRIDDLE CAKES (*Serves 4*)

Preparation and Cooking Time: 20 minutes

3 tablespoons peanut butter   2 cups Corn Wheat Griddle
1 cup milk   Cake Mix

In a bowl, mix peanut butter and milk until smooth. Stir in mix to form batter. Heat a lightly oiled griddle or heavy frying pan to medium hot. Drop batter onto griddle using a serving spoon or ladle. When the griddle cake surfaces are covered with bubbles, flip over and brown lightly on the second side. Serve with syrup or malt.

BREAKFAST CORN RAISIN MUFFINS (*Makes 12*)

Preparation and Baking Time: 25 minutes

¼ cup blackstrap molasses   ½ cup raisins
  1 egg   2 cups Corn Wheat Griddle
1¼ cups milk   Cake Mix
¼ cup corn oil

Preheat oven to 400 degrees.
In a bowl, beat blackstrap molasses, egg, milk and oil until well combined. Stir in raisins and mix to form a smooth batter.
Spoon batter into 12 well-oiled muffin cups. Bake for 20 minutes until golden brown.

BASIC RICE GRIDDLE CAKE MIX
(*Makes 2 quarts mix*)

5 cups brown rice flour   3 tablespoons non-alum baking
2 cups whole wheat pastry   powder
   flour   1 teaspoon salt (optional)
                   1 teaspoon ground cardamom

In a large bowl, combine all ingredients and mix thoroughly. Place in a half-gallon wide-mouth jar, seal tightly and store in cool dry cupboard. Use within two months.

RICE FLOUR PANCAKES (*Serves 4*)

Preparation and Cooking Time: 20 minutes

2 eggs   1 cup milk
2 cups Rice Griddle Cake Mix

In a bowl, beat together eggs and milk. Stir in mix until combined. Heat a lightly oiled griddle or heavy frying pan to medium hot. Drop batter onto griddle using a serving spoon or ladle. When the pancake surfaces are covered with bubbles, flip over and brown on the second side. Serve with malt or syrup and butter.

RICE MOLASSES PANCAKES (*Serves 4*)

Preparation and Cooking Time: 20 minutes

1 cup milk   2 tablespoons blackstrap
2 eggs   molasses
2 cups Rice Griddle Cake Mix

In a bowl, beat together milk, eggs and molasses. Stir in mix until combined. Heat a lightly oiled griddle or frying pan to medium hot. Drop batter onto griddle using a serving spoon or ladle. When pancake surfaces are covered with bubbles, flip over and lightly brown on the second side. Serve with a dab of butter or jam.

RICE APPLE GRIDDLE CAKES (Serves 4)

Preparation and Cooking Time: 20 minutes

1½ cups apple juice	2 cups Rice Griddle Cake
3 eggs	Mix
1 tablespoon oil	⅔ cup grated apple

In a bowl, beat together apple juice, eggs and oil. Stir in mix until moistened. Fold in grated apple until evenly distributed. Heat a lightly oiled griddle or heavy frying pan to medium hot. Drop batter onto griddle using a serving spoon or ladle. When pancake surfaces are covered with bubbles, flip over and brown lightly on the second side. Serve with syrup or applesauce.

RICE NUT BUTTER PANCAKES (Serves 4)

Preparation and Cooking Time: 20 minutes

1½ cups apple juice	2 eggs, beaten
4 tablespoons peanut,	1¾ cups Rice Griddle Cake
cashew or almond butter	Mix

In a bowl, beat together apple juice and nut butter until smooth. Beat in eggs. Stir in mix until combined. Heat a lightly oiled griddle to medium hot. Drop batter onto griddle using a serving spoon or ladle. When pancake surfaces are covered with bubbles, flip over and brown lightly on the second side. Serve with syrup or malt.

RICE FLOUR MORNING CAKE
(Makes 10-inch tube cake)

Preparation and Baking Time: 1¼ hours

NUT TOPPING INGREDIENTS

½ cup liquid barley malt
2 tablespoons oil
⅔ cup chopped nuts

½ cup shredded unsweetened
   coconut
¼ cup toasted wheat germ

CAKE INGREDIENTS

4 eggs
¼ cup oil or melted butter

1½ cups Rice Griddle Cake
   Mix

½ cup hot apple juice

Preheat oven to 325 degrees.

TOPPING

Heat malt and oil in a saucepan, stirring constantly, for 5 minutes. Remove from heat and stir in nuts, coconut and wheat germ until coated with malt mixture. Set aside.

CAKE

Beat eggs and oil or butter until lemon yellow in color. Add mix and apple juice alternately to egg mixture, beating constantly to form a smooth batter. Pour one-third cake batter into a well-oiled 10-inch tube pan. Dot with one-third of topping mixture. Pour in another third of cake batter and dot with a third of topping. Pour in final third of batter and dot the top of the cake with nut topping.

Bake for 1 hour or until done.

BASIC RAISIN COCONUT OATMEAL MIX
(Makes 1 quart mix)

3 cups rolled oats	½ cup shredded unsweetened
½ cup raisins or chopped	coconut
dates	½ teaspoon cinnamon
½ teaspoon ground cardamom	

In a large bowl, combine all ingredients and mix thoroughly. Place in a quart jar, seal tightly and store in cool dry cupboard. Use within two months.

RAISIN COCONUT OATMEAL CEREAL *(Serves 4)*

Preparation and Cooking Time: 10 minutes

4 cups water	1¾ cups Raisin Coconut Oatmeal Mix

In a saucepan, boil water. Gradually stir in mix. Continue to boil lightly, stirring occasionally, for 5 minutes until cereal reaches desired consistency.

This cereal may be served with milk, yogurt, fresh fruit or apple juice.

HIGH PROTEIN RAISIN COCONUT OATMEAL
(Serves 4)

Preparation and Cooking Time: 10 minutes

¼ cup dry milk powder	4 cups milk
1¼ cups Raisin Coconut Oatmeal Mix	1 egg, beaten

In a saucepan, combine milk powder and mix. Gradually stir in milk. Bring to a gentle boil and cook for 7 minutes, stirring occasionally, until cereal reaches desired consistency. Stir in egg and allow to cook for 2 more minutes.

This cereal may be served with yogurt, milk, cream, apple juice, fresh fruit or applesauce.

APPLE RAISIN COCONUT OATMEAL (*Serves 4*)

Preparation and Cooking Time: 10 minutes

1⅓ cups Raisin Coconut Oatmeal Mix	4 cups apple juice 1 cup chopped unpeeled apples

In a saucepan, combine mix, apple juice and chopped apples. Bring to a gentle boil and cook for 7 minutes until cereal reaches desired consistency.

This hot cereal may be served with milk, cream, yogurt or buttermilk.

FRIED OATMEAL SLICES (*Serves 4*)

Preparation and Cooking Time: 10 minutes

3 cups leftover cooked Raisin Coconut Oatmeal Cereal	1 teaspoon butter

Spoon leftover cereal into an oiled loaf pan. Cover with plastic wrap or foil and refrigerate overnight.

Loosen sides and slip cereal loaf out of pan as you would a loaf of bread. Slice molded oatmeal cereal into ½-inch thicknesses. Melt butter in a frying pan or griddle over medium heat. Fry slices until lightly browned on both sides.

OATMEAL FRENCH TOAST (*Serves 4*)

Preparation and Cooking Time: 15 minutes

3 cups leftover cooked Raisin Coconut Oatmeal Cereal	2 eggs 2 tablespoons milk
1 tablespoon butter	

Spoon leftover cereal into an oiled loaf pan. Cover with plastic wrap or foil and refrigerate overnight.

Loosen sides and slip cereal loaf out of pan as you would

a loaf of bread. Slice molded oatmeal cereal into ½-inch thicknesses.

In a shallow bowl, beat together eggs and milk. Melt butter in a heavy frying pan or griddle over medium heat. Dip cereal slices in egg mixture and fry until lightly browned on both sides, as you would French toast.

These slices may be served alone or with butter and syrup or a dab of sour cream.

OATMEAL BREAKFAST BARS (Makes 12)

Preparation and Cooking Time: 10 minutes

¼ cup buttter
1 cup liquid barley malt

2 cups Raisin Coconut Oatmeal Mix

In a saucepan, melt butter over medium heat. Stir in malt and cook for 3 minutes until malt is bubbling throughout. Remove from heat and stir in mix until thoroughly coated.

When mixture is cooled enough to handle, shape into breakfast bar shapes with moistened hands. Allow to cool and become crisp before serving.

OATMEAL MORNING COOKIES (Makes 12)

Preparation and Baking Time: 15 minutes

¼ cup butter
2 eggs
1 tablespoon blackstrap molasses

1 cup Raisin Coconut Oatmeal Mix
⅓ cup brown rice flour

Preheat oven to 350 degrees.

In a saucepan, melt butter. When cool beat in eggs and molasses. Stir in mix and flour to form dough.

Drop by spoonfuls onto well-oiled cookie sheet. Bake for 10 minutes until edges are lightly browned.

BASIC MALTED CRACKED WHEAT
CEREAL MIX (Makes 1 quart mix)

3 cups cracked wheat
⅓ cup chopped nuts
⅓ cup raisins or chopped
dates

¼ cup powdered malt*
1 teaspoon cinnamon
1 teaspoon cardamom seeds

In a large bowl, combine all ingredients and mix thoroughly. Place in a wide-mouth quart jar, seal tightly and store in cool dry cupboard. Use within two months if possible.

MALTED CRACKED WHEAT CEREAL (Serves 4)

Preparation and Cooking Time: 25 minutes

1 cup Malted Cracked Wheat
Cereal Mix

3 cups water

In a saucepan, combine mix and water. Bring to a gentle boil. Reduce heat to a simmer and cook for 20 minutes, stirring occasionally. Serve with milk, cream, yogurt, buttermilk, fresh fruit or applesauce.

CRACKED WHEAT CREAM CEREAL (Serves 4)

Preparation and Cooking Time: 30 minutes

1 cup Malted Cracked
Wheat Cereal Mix

1½ cups water
2 cups milk

In a saucepan, combine mix and water. Bring to a boil and continue to boil for 5 minutes, stirring occasionally. Reduce heat to a simmer and stir in milk. Cook for 20 minutes until cereal is soft and creamy. Serve with fresh fruit, raisins, dates or chopped nuts.

---

* Available at health and natural food stores.

MALTED APPLE CRACKED WHEAT CEREAL
(Serves 4)

Preparation and Cooking Time: 30 minutes

1 cup Malted Cracked Wheat
Cereal Mix

3 cups apple juice
2 apples, finely chopped

In a saucepan, combine mix and apple juice. Cover pan and bring to a gentle boil. Add apples and reduce heat. Simmer for 25 minutes until cereal is soft. Serve with milk, cream, buttermilk, yogurt or chopped nuts.

MORNING WHEAT COOKIES (Makes 12)

Preparation and Baking Time: 25 minutes

2 cups leftover cooked
Malted Cracked Wheat
Cereal (p. 26)

1 cup whole wheat flour
¼ cup sesame oil
1 egg, beaten

Preheat oven to 350 degrees.
In a bowl, combine all ingredients to make a stiff dough. With moistened hands form tablespoons of dough into balls and place 1½ inches apart on an oiled cookie sheet. Press flat with a wet fork. Bake for 15 to 20 minutes until golden brown.

CRACKED WHEAT BREAKFAST LOAF (Serves 4)

Preparation and Cooking Time: 20 minutes

3 cups leftover cooked
Malted Cracked Wheat
Cereal (p. 26)

⅔ cup whole wheat flour
1 egg, beaten
1 tablespoon butter

In a bowl, mix leftover cereal with flour and egg. Spoon into a well-oiled loaf pan. Cover with plastic wrap or foil and refrigerate overnight.

Remove molded loaf from pan as you would a loaf of bread. Slice into ½-inch thicknesses. Melt butter in a heavy frying pan or griddle over medium heat. Fry wheat slices on both sides until lightly browned. Serve with syrup and butter or with a dab of sour cream or yogurt.

BASIC SPICED MILLET PORRIDGE MIX
(*Makes 1 quart mix*)

3¼ cups millet
 ⅔ cup raisins or chopped
      dates

½ teaspoon cinnamon
½ teaspoon ground ginger
1 teaspoon cardamom seeds

½ teaspoon ground cloves

In a large bowl, combine all ingredients and mix thoroughly. Place in a quart jar, seal tightly and store in cool dry cupboard. Use within two months.

SPICED MILLET PORRIDGE (*Serves 4*)

Preparation and Cooking Time: 30 minutes

1 cup Spiced Millet Porridge
  Mix

4 cups water

In a saucepan, combine mix and water. Cover and bring to a gentle boil. Reduce heat to a simmer and cook for 25 minutes. Serve with milk, yogurt, cream, fresh fruit or applesauce.

CREAMED MILLET PORRIDGE (Serves 4)

Preparation and Cooking Time: 35 minutes

1 cup Spiced Millet   2½ cups water
Porridge Mix   1½ cups milk

In a saucepan, combine mix and water. Bring to a boil and reduce heat to low. Add milk, cover and simmer for 30 minutes until soft.

Puree cooked cereal in a blender or food processor until smooth. Serve with milk, cream, yogurt, buttermilk or fresh fruit.

MILKY MILLET PORRIDGE (Serves 4)

Preparation and Cooking Time: 35 minutes

1 cup Spiced Millet Porridge   2 cups water
Mix   2 cups milk

In a saucepan, combine mix and water. Bring to a boil. Add milk and reduce heat. Cover and simmer for 25 minutes until soft. Stir occasionally to prevent sticking. Serve with fresh fruit, nuts or applesauce.

APPLE MILLET PORRIDGE (Serves 4)

Preparation and Cooking Time: 30 minutes

1 cup Spiced Millet   3½ cups apple juice
Porridge Mix   ¾ cup chopped apples

In a saucepan, combine mix and apple juice. Bring to a boil. Stir in apples and cover. Reduce heat and simmer for 25 minutes, stirring occasionally.

Serve with chopped nuts, milk, cream, yogurt or buttermilk.

MILLET BREAKFAST PATTIES (*Serves 4*)

Preparation and Cooking Time: 20 minutes

3 cups cooked leftover Spiced ⅔ cup whole wheat pastry
Millet Porridge (p. 28)   flour
¼ cup tahini*

In a bowl, combine cooked millet porridge, flour and tahini to form a stiff dough.

With moistened hands, shape dough into patties. Heat a well-oiled heavy frying pan or griddle over medium heat. Brown patties lightly on both sides. Serve alone or with applesauce.

BRAN FLAKES (*Makes 1½ quarts*)

Preparation and Baking Time: 1 hour

2½ cups bran   ½ cup whole wheat flour
3½ cups water

Preheat oven to 325 degrees.

In a bowl, combine bran, flour and water to make a thin batter.

Pour 1 cup batter into each of 3 well-oiled cookie sheets. Bake for 45 minutes until dry and crisp.

Crumble between fingers and store in a wide-mouth jar. Seal tightly. Remains crisp two weeks. Serve with milk, yogurt, buttermilk, soy milk, or apple juice and fresh fruit.

---

* Tahini is a seed butter made from sesame seeds. It is a common Middle Eastern food and can be readily found at specialty shops, and in health and natural food stores.

VARIETY FLAKE GRANOLA (*Makes 2 quarts*)

Preparation and Baking Time: 30 minutes

2 cups rolled oats
1½ cups rye flakes
1¼ cups wheat flakes
½ cup wheat germ
1 cup shredded unsweet-
    ened coconut

⅔ cup chopped nuts or
    sunflower seeds
¼ cup butter
2 tablespoons blackstrap
    molasses
⅔ cup liquid barley malt

1 cup raisins or chopped dates

Preheat oven to 325 degrees.

In a large bowl, combine oats, rye flakes, wheat flakes, wheat germ, coconut and nuts or seeds.

In a saucepan, heat butter, molasses and malt until combined and liquefied. Stir in oat mixture and spread on oiled cookie sheet.

Bake for 20 minutes until lightly browned and crisp. Stir in raisins or dates and store in a tightly covered jar.

Variety Flake Granola may be eaten with milk, buttermilk, apple juice or soy milk and fresh fruit.

SESAME BUCKWHEAT GRANOLA (*Makes 2 quarts*)

Preparation and Baking Time: 30 minutes

3¼ cups rolled oats
1½ cups buckwheat groats
    (kasha)
¾ cup sesame seeds

½ cup chopped almonds
3 tablespoons butter
½ cup liquid barley malt
½ cup raisins

Preheat oven to 325 degrees.

In a large bowl, combine oats, buckwheat groats, sesame seeds and almonds.

In a saucepan, melt butter. Stir in malt and cook for 2 minutes until liquefied. Pour over oat mixture and toss until well coated. Spread thickly on lightly oiled baking sheets and bake for 20 minutes until lightly browned and crisp. Stir in raisins and store in a tightly covered jar. Serve with milk, yogurt, buttermilk, apple juice or soy milk and fresh fruit.

COCONUT RAISIN GRANOLA (Makes 2 quarts)

Preparation and Baking Time: 30 minutes

5 cups rolled oats	3 tablespoons butter
1 cup wheat germ	½ cup liquid barley malt
1 cup shredded unsweetened coconut	2 tablespoons blackstrap molasses

¾ cup raisins or currants

Preheat oven to 325 degrees.

In a large bowl, combine oats, wheat germ, and coconut.

In a saucepan, melt butter. Stir in malt and molasses. Cook until liquefied. Pour over oat mixture and toss until evenly coated.

Bake for 20 minutes on oiled baking sheets until lightly browned and crisp. Add raisins or currants and store in a tightly covered jar. Serve with milk, buttermilk, yogurt, apple juice or soy milk and fresh fruit.

MALTED WHEAT CAKES (Makes 2 quarts)

Preparation and Cooking Time: 20 minutes

1 6-ounce package wheat puffs or Puffed Wheat	1 cup chopped nuts
	3 tablespoons butter

½ cup liquid barley malt

In a bowl, mix puffed wheat and nuts.

In a saucepan, melt butter over medium heat and stir in malt. Continue stirring while mixture boils for 3 minutes. Pour hot malt over puffed wheat and nuts. Toss until puffed wheat is evenly coated with malt. When mixture is cool enough to handle, moisten hands and shape into small teaspoon-sized balls.

Store in a wide-mouth jar and seal tightly. This cereal will remain fresh for two weeks.

Malted wheat cakes can be munched on as a snack or eaten with milk, buttermilk or soy milk and fresh fruit as a cold breakfast cereal.

MOLASSES, WHEAT GERM, RAISINS AND NUT CEREAL (Makes 1 quart)

Preparation and Cooking Time: 15 minutes

3 cups toasted wheat germ
½ cup raisins
½ cup chopped nuts
2 tablespoons butter
¼ cup liquid barley malt
1 tablespoon blackstrap molasses

In a bowl, mix wheat germ, raisins and nuts until well combined.

In a saucepan, melt butter over medium heat. Stir in malt and molasses. Cook, stirring constantly, for 3 minutes while malt and molasses boil. Pour hot malt molasses mixture over wheat germ mixture. Toss until well coated.

Store cereal in a wide-mouth jar and seal tightly. Can be kept for three weeks with little loss of freshness. Serve with milk, yogurt, buttermilk or apple juice and fresh fruit.

SWEET WHEAT PUFFS (Makes 2½ quarts)

Preparation and Cooking Time: 15 minutes

2 tablespoons butter
⅔ cup liquid barley malt
1 6-ounce package wheat puffs or Puffed Wheat

In a large pot, melt butter over medium heat. Stir in malt. Cook, stirring constantly, for 3 minutes while malt boils. Gradually add puffed wheat while stirring to coat wheat uniformly. Remove from heat and cool. Store in a wide-mouth jar and seal tightly. This cereal will stay fresh for three weeks.

CHAPTER THREE

Light Soup and Gravy Mixes

Every homemade mix in this chapter can be stored for two months in a cool dark cabinet with little loss of flavor. Most can be prepared in under 15 minutes by adding water, tomato juice or milk. Each will provide a variety of possibilities. We suggest making soups in individual serving portions, since often a quick soup is needed for just one person. However, to make mixes in more bulk, recipes can easily be multiplied.

Only whole grains, whole grain flours and pastas are used in these soup mixes since they provide a wider and greater spectrum of nutrients than refined flours, grains and pastas. All these products are readily available at health and natural food stores. Often, leftover grains or legumes and fresh vegetables are suggested as quick additions to soup in order to vary the taste and increase the dietary value.

Many light soups also double as gravy mixes. These gravies can be used to add interest to steamed vegetables, cooked grains and main dishes. By keeping several containers of homemade soup and gravy mixes on your shelves your menus for both lunches and dinners will be enhanced.

BASIC CREAM OF ONION SOUP MIX
(Makes 1 quart mix)

1¼ cups whole wheat pastry flour
1¼ cups non-instant powdered milk
⅔ cup dried onion
2 teaspoons black pepper

1 teaspoon garlic powder
⅓ cup dried parsley
1 teaspoon salt (optional)
⅓ cup powdered vegetable broth

In a bowl, combine all ingredients and mix thoroughly. Place in a wide-mouth quart jar, seal tightly and store in cool dark cupboard. Use within two months.

CREAM OF ONION SOUP *(Serves 1)*

Preparation and Cooking Time: 12 minutes

¼ cup Cream of Onion Soup Mix
1 cup milk

In a saucepan, beat mix and milk until well combined. Cook over medium heat, stirring occasionally, for 10 minutes until soup thickens. Serve alone or topped with grated cheese or croutons.

TOMATO ONION CREAM SOUP *(Serves 1)*

Preparation and Cooking Time: 12 minutes

¼ cup Cream of Onion Soup Mix
1 cup milk
1 teaspoon tomato paste

In a saucepan, beat mix and milk until well combined. Cook over medium heat, stirring occasionally, for 10 minutes until soup has thickened. Beat in tomato paste with a wire whisk. Serve with crackers or croutons or topped with grated cheese.

CORN CHOWDER (Serves 1)

Preparation and Cooking Time: 12 minutes

¼ cup Cream of Onion Soup   1 cup milk
Mix   ¼ cup corn kernels

In a saucepan, beat mix and milk until well combined. Stir in corn. Cook over medium heat for 10 minutes, stirring occasionally to prevent lumps. Serve alone or with crackers and topped with grated cheese.

POTATO CHOWDER (Serves 1)

Preparation and Cooking Time: 12 minutes

¼ cup Cream of Onion Soup   ¼ cup diced leftover boiled
Mix   potato
1 cup milk

In a saucepan, beat mix and milk until well combined. Stir in diced potato. Cook over medium heat, stirring occasionally to prevent lumps, for 10 minutes until chowder has thickened. Serve alone or with crackers.

RICE CHOWDER (Serves 1)

Preparation and Cooking Time: 12 minutes

¼ cup Cream of Onion Soup   1 cup milk
Mix   ¼ cup cooked brown rice

In a saucepan, beat mix and milk until well combined. Stir in rice. Cook over medium heat, stirring occasionally to prevent lumps, for 10 minutes until chowder has thickened. Serve alone, with crackers or topped with grated cheese.

ONION CREAM SAUCE (Makes 1 cup)

Preparation and Cooking Time: 12 minutes

⅓ cup Cream of Onion Soup   1 cup milk
  Mix

In a saucepan, beat mix and milk until well combined. Cook over medium heat for 10 minutes, stirring occasionally to prevent lumps.

When sauce has thickened, it may be served on noodles, rice, boiled potatoes, steamed vegetables or fish.

BASIC CLEAR ONION SOUP MIX
(*Makes 2 cups mix*)

1 cup dark miso paste   1 cup dried minced onion

In a bowl or food processor cream miso and onion until well combined. Spoon into a wide-mouth jar, seal tightly and store in cool dry cupboard for one month.

CLEAR ONION SOUP (Serves 1)

Preparation and Cooking Time: 10 minutes

1 tablespoon Clear Onion   1 cup water
  Soup Mix

In a saucepan, dissolve mix in water. Cook over medium heat without boiling for 8 minutes. Serve alone or with crackers.

FRENCH ONION SOUP (Serves 1)

Preparation and Cooking Time: 15 minutes

1 tablespoon Clear Onion
Soup Mix
1 cup water

1 slice whole grain bread
⅓ cup grated mozzarella
cheese

In a saucepan, dissolve mix in water. Cook over medium heat without boiling for 8 minutes.

While soup cooks, toast bread and cut it into a 3½-inch circle using a cookie cutter or English muffin ring.

Pour soup into a single-serving casserole dish, place toasted bread in dish and top with grated cheese.

Place casserole under broiler for 5 minutes until cheese is melted. Serve as a luncheon dish or as an appetizer.

ONION TOMATO SOUP (Serves 1)

Preparation and Cooking Time: 10 minutes

1 tablespoon Clear Onion
Soup Mix

1 cup tomato juice

In a saucepan, dissolve mix in tomato juice. Cook over medium heat without boiling for 8 minutes. Serve alone or with crackers, croutons or grated cheese added.

ONION BUTTERMILK SOUP (Serves 1)

Preparation and Cooking Time: 10 minutes

1 tablespoon Clear Onion
Soup Mix

1 cup buttermilk

In a saucepan, dissolve mix in buttermilk. Cook over medium-low heat, stirring occasionally, for 8 minutes. Serve alone or with croutons.

ONION VEGETABLE SOUP (Serves 1)

Preparation and Cooking Time: 15 minutes

1 tablespoon Clear Onion Soup Mix	¼ cup chopped vegetables (carrots, parsley, celery,
1 cup tomato juice	spinach and/or squash)

In a saucepan, dissolve mix in tomato juice. Stir in vegetables. Cook over medium heat for 8 minutes without boiling. Serve alone or topped with croutons or grated cheese.

PUREED ONION VEGETABLE SOUP (Serves 1)

Preparation and Cooking Time: 15 minutes

1 tablespoon Clear Onion Soup Mix	⅓ cup chopped green vegetables (spinach,
1 cup water	broccoli and/or zucchini

1 tablespoon sour cream

In a saucepan, dissolve mix in water. Stir in vegetables. Cook over medium heat without boiling for 8 minutes.

Remove from heat, add sour cream, and puree in an electric blender or food processor until smooth. Serve alone or with croutons.

BROWN ONION GRAVY (Makes 1 cup)

Preparation and Cooking Time: 10 minutes

1 tablespoon Clear Onion Soup Mix	1½ teaspoons arrowroot starch dissolved in 1 tablespoon
1 cup water	water

In a saucepan, dissolve mix in water. Cook over medium-high heat nearly to boiling. Stir in starch-and-water combination. Continue stirring for 3 minutes until gravy has thickened. Serve on grain or main dishes.

BASIC CREAM OF MUSHROOM SOUP MIX
(Makes 1 quart mix)

1½ cups whole wheat pastry
     flour
1⅓ cups non-instant powdered
     milk
¾   cup dried mushrooms

3 tablespoons dried minced
   onion
3 tablespoons dried parsley
1 teaspoon dried minced
   garlic

1 teaspoon salt or salt substitute

In a bowl, combine all ingredients and mix thoroughly. Place in a wide-mouth jar, seal tightly and store in cool dark cupboard. Use within two months.

CREAM OF MUSHROOM SOUP *(Serves 1)*

Preparation and Cooking Time: 10 minutes

¼ cup Cream of Mushroom   1 cup milk
   Soup Mix

In a saucepan, beat mix and milk until well combined. Cook over medium heat, stirring occasionally, for 8 minutes until soup thickens, and mushrooms are tender.

MUSHROOM BISQUE *(Serves 1)*

Preparation and Cooking Time: 10 minutes

¼ cup Cream of Mushroom   1 cup light cream
   Soup Mix   1 teaspoon tomato paste

In a saucepan, combine mix and cream, beating with a wire whisk. Cook over medium heat for 8 minutes, stirring occasionally, until soup has thickened and mushrooms are tender.

Using a wire whisk, beat in tomato paste. Cook for 2 minutes without boiling before serving. Best served alone, either hot or cold.

CREAM OF MUSHROOM AND CELERY SOUP
(Serves 1)

Preparation and Cooking Time: 10 minutes

¼ cup Cream of Mushroom   1 cup milk
Soup Mix   ¼ cup chopped celery

In a saucepan, beat mix and milk until well combined. Stir in celery. Cook over medium heat, stirring occasionally, for 8 minutes until soup has thickened and mushrooms are tender. Serve alone or topped with grated cheese or croutons.

MUSHROOM RICE SOUP (Serves 1)

Preparation and Cooking Time: 12 minutes

¼ cup Cream of Mushroom   1 cup milk
Soup Mix   ¼ cup cooked brown rice

In a saucepan, beat mix with milk until well combined. Stir in rice. Cook over medium heat, stirring occasionally, for 10 minutes until soup thickens and mushrooms are tender. Serve alone, with croutons or topped with grated cheese.

PUMPKIN MUSHROOM SOUP OR SAUCE
(Serves 1 or makes 1 cup)

Preparation and Cooking Time: 10 minutes

¼ cup Cream of Mushroom   ¾ cup water
Soup Mix   ¼ cup pureed pumpkin

In a saucepan, beat mix, water and pumpkin until well combined. Cook over medium heat, stirring occasionally, for 8 minutes until soup thickens and mushrooms are tender.

MUSHROOM CREAM GRAVY (*Makes 1 cup*)

Preparation and Cooking Time: 10 minutes

⅓ cup Cream of Mushroom   ¾ cup milk
Soup Mix   ¼ cup heavy cream

In a saucepan, beat mix, milk and cream until well combined. Cook over medium-high heat for 8 minutes, stirring occasionally, until thickened and mushrooms are tender. Serve over grain, potatoes, steamed vegetables or fish.

BASIC LIGHT BROWN MUSHROOM SOUP MIX
(*Makes 1 quart mix*)

1 cup whole wheat pastry flour
1 cup soybean or chick-pea flour
1 cup dark miso paste
¾ cup dried mushrooms

½ teaspoon black pepper
2 tablespoons nutritional yeast
2 tablespoons ground cumin
1 tablespoon ground coriander

In a large bowl or food processor combine all ingredients and mix thoroughly. Mixture will have the texture of fine oatmeal. Spoon into a wide-mouth jar, seal tightly and store in cool dry cupboard. Use within three weeks.

LIGHT BROWN MUSHROOM SOUP (*Serves 1*)

Preparation and Cooking Time: 10 minutes

2 tablespoons Light Brown   1 cup water
Mushroom Soup Mix

In a saucepan, combine mix with water, using a wire whisk. Cook over medium heat, stirring occasionally to prevent lumps, for 8 minutes until soup thickens and mushrooms are tender. Serve alone or topped with croutons.

TOMATO MUSHROOM SOUP (Serves 1)

Preparation and Cooking Time: 10 minutes

2 tablespoons Light Brown   1 cup tomato juice
Mushroom Soup Mix

In a saucepan, combine mix and tomato juice, using a wire whisk. Cook over medium heat, stirring occasionally to prevent lumps, for 8 minutes until soup thickens and mushrooms are tender. Serve alone, with croutons or topped with grated cheese.

VEGETABLE MUSHROOM SOUP (Serves 1)

Preparation and Cooking Time: 16 minutes

¾ cup water   2 tablespoons Light Brown
¼ cup chopped vegetables   Mushroom Soup Mix
   (parsley, celery, carrots,   dissolved in 3 tablespoons
   squash and/or broccoli)   water

In a saucepan, combine water and vegetables. Cook, covered, over medium heat without boiling for 5 minutes.
Stir in mix-and-water paste. Cook an additional 10 minutes, stirring occasionally to prevent lumps from forming. When thickened, this soup may be served alone, or topped with croutons or grated cheese.

LIGHT BROWN MUSHROOM RICE SOUP (Serves 1)

Preparation and Cooking Time: 10 minutes

2 tablespoons Light Brown   1 cup water
Mushroom Soup Mix   ¼ cup cooked brown rice

In a saucepan, combine mix with water, using a wire whisk. Stir in rice. Cook over medium heat, stirring occasionally to prevent lumps, for 8 minutes until soup thickens and mushrooms are tender. Serve alone or topped with croutons.

LIGHT BROWN MUSHROOM GRAVY (Makes 1 cup)

Preparation and Cooking Time: 10 minutes

5 tablespoons Light Brown
Mushroom Soup Mix

1 cup water

In a saucepan, beat mix and water with a wire whisk. Cook over medium heat, stirring occasionally to prevent lumps, for 8 minutes until gravy thickens and mushrooms are tender. Serve with grains, steamed vegetables or boiled potatoes.

TOMATO MUSHROOM CREAM SAUCE (Makes 1 cup)

Preparation and Cooking Time: 10 minutes

5 tablespoons Light Brown
Mushroom Soup Mix

1 cup tomato juice

In a saucepan, combine mix with juice, using a wire whisk. Cook over medium heat, stirring occasionally to prevent lumps, for 8 minutes. When gravy thickens it can be served with cooked grains, pastas, steamed vegetables or fish.

BASIC ABC SOUP MIX
(*Makes 1 quart mix*)

2½ cups whole wheat ABC
pasta
1¼ cups dehydrated vegetable
flakes
1 tablespoon dried minced
onion

1 tablespoon dried parsley
½ teaspoon black pepper
2 teaspoons salt (optional)
1 teaspoon oregano

In a bowl, combine all ingredients and mix thoroughly. Place in a wide-mouth jar, seal tightly and store in cool dark cupboard. Will stay fresh for two months or longer.

ABC SOUP (Serves 1)

Preparation and Cooking Time: 15 minutes

⅔ cup water   3 tablespoons ABC Soup Mix
⅓ cup tomato juice

In a saucepan, bring water to a boil. Shake jar of ABC Soup Mix and measure 3 tablespoons into water. Boil gently for 10 minutes until pasta and vegetables are tender. Reduce heat to low and stir in tomato juice. Simmer for 2 minutes until soup is heated. Serve alone, with crackers, croutons or topped with grated cheese.

CREAM OF ABC SOUP (Serves 1)

Preparation and Cooking Time: 15 minutes

⅔ cup water   1 teaspoon arrowroot starch
3 tablespoons ABC Soup Mix   mixed with ⅓ cup milk

In a saucepan, bring water to a boil. Shake jar of ABC Soup Mix and measure 3 tablespoons into water. Boil for 7 minutes until vegetables and pasta are tender. Stir in starch-and-milk mixture. Continue stirring for 3 minutes until soup thickens. Serve alone, with crackers, croutons or topped with grated cheese.

TAMARI BROTH ABC SOUP (Serves 1)

Preparation and Cooking Time: 10 minutes

1 cup water   3 tablespoons ABC Soup Mix
½ teaspoon tamari soy sauce

In a saucepan, bring water to a boil. Shake jar of ABC Soup Mix and measure 3 tablespoons mix into water. Boil for 7 minutes until vegetables and pasta are tender. Stir in soy sauce. Serve alone, with crackers, croutons or topped with grated cheese.

NON-DAIRY ABC SOUP (Serves 1)

Preparation and Cooking Time: 15 minutes

1 cup water
3 tablespoons ABC Soup Mix

1 teaspoon soy flour dissolved
in 1 tablespoon water

In a saucepan, bring water to a boil. Shake jar of ABC Soup Mix and measure 3 tablespoons into water. Boil for 7 minutes until vegetables and pasta are tender. Stir soy-flour paste into boiling soup. Cook, stirring constantly, for 5 minutes until soup thickens. Serve with crackers or croutons.

ABC BEAN SOUP (Serves 1)

Preparation and Cooking Time: 10 minutes

1 cup water
3 tablespoons ABC Soup Mix

3 tablespoons cooked beans
1 teaspoon tomato paste

In a saucepan, bring water to a boil. Shake jar of ABC Soup Mix and measure 3 tablespoons into water. Add beans and boil for 7 minutes until pasta and vegetables are tender. Stir in tomato paste until dissolved. Serve alone or topped with grated cheese.

BASIC JAPANESE SEAWEED SOUP MIX
(Makes 2 cups mix)

1 cup hiziki seaweed
1 cup miso paste
2 tablespoons dried chives

2 tablespoons dried minced
onion

Break seaweed between fingers into ¼-inch lengths. In a bowl, cream seaweed, miso paste, chives and onion until well combined. Spoon mixture into a wide-mouth jar and seal. Will remain fresh without refrigeration for one month.

JAPANESE SEAWEED SOUP (Serves 1)

Preparation and Cooking Time: 10 minutes

1 tablespoon Japanese Seaweed Soup Mix	1 cup water

In a saucepan, combine mix and water until miso is dissolved. Cook over medium heat, without boiling, for 8 minutes, until seaweed is tender.

This soup should be served while still hot.

SEAWEED SESAME RICE SOUP (Serves 1)

Preparation and Cooking Time: 10 minutes

1 tablespoon Japanese Seaweed Soup Mix	1 cup water 1 tablespoon tahini

In a saucepan, combine mix and water until miso is dissolved. Cook over medium heat, without boiling, for 8 minutes until seaweed is tender. Beat in tahini with a wire whisk until smooth.

This soup is best served hot.

SEAWEED RICE SOUP (Serves 1)

Preparation and Cooking Time: 10 minutes

1 tablespoon Japanese Seaweed Soup Mix	3 tablespoons cooked rice 1 cup water

In a saucepan, combine mix, rice and water until miso is dissolved. Cook over medium heat, without boiling, for 8 minutes until seaweed is tender. Best served hot.

SEAWEED TOFU SOUP (Serves 1)

Preparation and Cooking Time: 10 minutes

1 tablespoon Japanese
Seaweed Soup Mix

1 cup water
¼ cup tofu, cut in cubes

In a saucepan, combine mix and water until miso is dissolved. Gently stir in tofu. Cook over medium heat, without boiling, for 8 minutes until seaweed is tender. Best served hot.

SEAWEED NOODLE SOUP (Serves 1)

Preparation and Cooking Time: 10 minutes

1 cup water
2 tablespoons soba, broken in
2-inch pieces

1 tablespoon Japanese
Seaweed Soup Mix

In a saucepan, bring water to a boil. Add soba to boiling water. Boil for 5 minutes.

Reduce heat to medium. When boiling subsides, stir in mix, until miso is dissolved. Cook for 5 minutes until seaweed is tender.

SEAWEED SAUCE (Makes 1 cup)

Preparation and Cooking Time: 10 minutes

1 tablespoon Japanese
Seaweed Soup Mix
1 cup water

1½ teaspoons arrowroot starch
dissolved in 2 teaspoons
water

In a saucepan, combine mix and water until miso is dissolved. Cook over medium heat, without boiling, for 8 minutes until seaweed is tender.

Stir in starch-and-water paste. Continue stirring for 2 minutes until sauce thickens. Serve over rice, noodles or steamed vegetables.

BASIC HERB BROTH MIX
(Makes 2 cups mix)

¾ cup nutritional yeast	2 tablespoons coriander seeds
½ cup dried minced onion	1 tablespoon turmeric
⅓ cup dried parsley	2 teaspoons ground cumin
2 tablespoons dried chives	1 teaspoon tarragon
2 teaspoons salt (optional)	

In a bowl, combine all ingredients and mix thoroughly. Place in wide-mouth jar, seal tightly and store in cool dark cupboard. Use within two months.

HERB BROTH *(Serves 1)*

Preparation and Cooking Time: 10 minutes

2 teaspoons Herb Broth Mix   1 cup water

In a saucepan, combine mix and water. Cook over medium heat for 8 minutes without boiling. Serve alone or with crackers or croutons.

TOMATO HERB SOUP *(Serves 1)*

Preparation and Cooking Time: 10 minutes

2 teaspoons Herb Broth Mix   1 cup tomato juice

In a saucepan, combine mix and tomato juice. Cook over medium-low heat for 8 minutes without boiling. Serve alone, or topped with croutons or grated cheese.

BUTTERMILK HERB SOUP *(Serves 1)*

Preparation and Cooking Time: 10 minutes

2 teaspoons Herb Broth Mix   1 cup buttermilk

In a saucepan, combine mix and buttermilk. Cook over medium-low heat for 8 minutes until flavors are well combined. Serve hot or cold.

CARROT HERB SOUP (Serves 1)

Preparation and Cooking Time: 10 minutes

2 teaspoons Herb Broth Mix   1 cup carrot juice

In a saucepan, combine mix and carrot juice. Cook over medium heat for 8 minutes without boiling. Serve alone or topped with croutons.

HERB VEGETABLE SOUP (Serves 1)

Preparation and Cooking Time: 10 minutes

2 teaspoons Herb Broth Mix   ¼ cup chopped vegetables
1 cup water or tomato juice   (carrots, squash, celery,
                                       peas and corn)

In a saucepan, combine mix, water or tomato juice and mixed vegetables. Cook over medium heat for 8 minutes, without boiling, until vegetables are cooked. Serve alone or topped with croutons or grated cheese.

HERB NOODLE SOUP (Serves 1)

Preparation and Cooking Time: 15 minutes

1 cup water   2 tablespoons whole grain
                                noodles
2 teaspoons Herb Broth Mix

In a saucepan, bring water to a boil. Add noodles and boil for 8 minutes until tender.

Reduce heat to medium. When boiling subsides, stir in mix until combined. Cook for 5 additional minutes. Serve alone or topped with croutons or grated cheese.

NON-DAIRY HERB CREAM SOUP *(Serves 1)*

Preparation and Cooking Time: 10 minutes

2 teaspoons Herb Broth Mix   1 cup water
4 teaspoons whole wheat
  pastry flour

In a saucepan, combine mix, flour and water, using a wire whisk. Cook over medium heat, stirring occasionally, for 5 minutes until soup thickens. Serve alone or topped with croutons.

HERB SAUCE *(Makes 1 cup)*

Preparation and Cooking Time: 10 minutes

2 teaspoons Herb Broth Mix   1 cup water or milk
2 tablespoons whole wheat   1 teaspoon butter
  pastry flour

In a saucepan, combine mix, flour and water or milk, using a wire whisk. Add butter. Cook over medium heat, stirring occasionally, for 8 minutes until thickened. Serve over grain, noodles, vegetables or fish.

BASIC DARK BROTH MIX
(Makes 2 cups mix)

1¼ cups miso paste   1 tablespoon ground cumin
½ cup dried minced onion   1 tablespoon ground
 1 tablespoon dried chives   coriander
 1 tablespoon dried minced   1 teaspoon black pepper
   garlic

In a bowl, cream miso paste with other ingredients until well distributed. Spoon into a wide-mouth jar, seal and store in cool dark cabinet. Use within one month.

DARK CONSOMMÉ (Serves 1)

Preparation and Cooking Time: 10 minutes

2 teaspoons Dark Broth Mix   1 cup water

In a saucepan, combine mix with water until miso is dissolved. Cook over medium heat for 8 minutes without boiling. Serve alone or topped with croutons.

TOMATO BROTH (Serves 1)

Preparation and Cooking Time: 10 minutes

2 teaspoons Dark Broth Mix   1 cup tomato juice

In a saucepan, combine mix and juice until miso is dissolved. Cook over medium heat for 8 minutes without boiling. Serve alone or topped with croutons or grated cheese.

CARROT BROTH (Serves 1)

Preparation and Cooking Time: 10 minutes

2 teaspoons Dark Broth Mix   1 cup carrot juice

In a saucepan, combine mix and juice until miso is dissolved. Cook over medium heat for 8 minutes without boiling. Serve alone or topped with croutons.

NOODLES IN DARK BROTH (Serves 1)

Preparation and Cooking Time: 15 minutes

1 cup water   2 tablespoons whole grain
                                            noodles
                2 teaspoons Dark Broth Mix

In a saucepan, bring water to a boil. Add noodles to boiling water. Cook for 8 minutes until tender.

Reduce heat to medium. When boiling subsides, stir in mix until dissolved. Cook for 5 minutes longer. Serve alone or topped with croutons.

DARK BROTH VEGETABLE SOUP (Serves 1)

Preparation and Cooking Time: 10 minutes

2 teaspoons Dark Broth Mix
1 cup water

¼ cup chopped vegetables
(celery, squash, green peppers, peas and/or corn)

In a saucepan, combine mix and water until miso dissolves. Stir in vegetables. Cook over medium heat for 8 minutes without boiling, until vegetables are cooked but still crisp. Serve alone or topped with croutons or grated cheese.

DARK BROWN GRAVY (Makes 1 cup)

Preparation and Cooking Time: 10 minutes

2 teaspoons Dark Broth Mix
1 cup water

2 teaspoons arrowroot starch dissolved in 1 tablespoon water

In a saucepan, combine mix and water until miso dissolves. Cook over medium heat for 8 minutes without boiling. Stir in starch-and-water paste. Continue stirring until gravy thickens. Serve over grains, noodles, tofu dishes or vegetables.

LIGHT BROWN GRAVY (Makes 1 cup)

Preparation and Cooking Time: 10 minutes

2 teaspoons Dark Broth Mix
1 cup water

2 tablespoons whole wheat pastry flour

In a saucepan, combine mix, water and flour until miso is dissolved and flour has no lumps. Cook over medium heat for 8 minutes, stirring occasionally, until gravy has thickened. Serve over grains, noodles or vegetables.

BASIC NUT AND RAISIN SOUP MIX
(*Makes 1 quart mix*)

2 cups raisins
½ cup arrowroot starch
½ cup coarsely chopped almonds
⅓ cup coarsely chopped pecans or walnuts
¼ cup cashew pieces

¼ cup coarsely chopped filberts
2 teaspoons dried lemon or orange peel
1 teaspoon cinnamon
1 teaspoon ground cardamom
½ teaspoon ground cloves

In a large bowl, combine all ingredients and mix thoroughly. Place in a wide-mouth jar, seal tightly and store in cool dry cupboard. Will retain its flavor for two months.

SWEET AND SOUR SOUP (*Serves 1*)

Preparation and Cooking Time: 5 minutes

1 cup water

3 tablespoons Nut and Raisin Soup Mix dissolved in 3 tablespoons water

In a saucepan, bring water to a boil. Stir in mix-and-water combination. Continue stirring for 3 minutes until soup thickens. Serve alone or with lemon slices floating on top.

SWEET CREAM SOUP (Serves 1)

Preparation and Cooking Time: 5 minutes

1 cup milk

3 tablespoons Nut and Raisin Soup Mix dissolved in 3 tablespoons light cream

In a saucepan, bring milk to a gentle boil. Add mix-and-cream combination. Stir for 3 minutes until soup thickens. Serve hot or cold.

NUTTY TOMATO SOUP (Serves 1)

Preparation and Cooking Time: 5 minutes

1 cup tomato juice

3 tablespoons Nut and Raisin Soup Mix dissolved in 3 tablespoons tomato juice

In a saucepan, bring juice to a gentle boil. Add mix-and-juice combination. Stir for 3 minutes until soup thickens. Serve hot or cold.

SWEET AND SOUR RICE SOUP (Serves 1)

Preparation and Cooking Time: 5 minutes

1 cup tomato juice
3 tablespoons Nut and Raisin Soup Mix dissolved in 3 tablespoons water

¼ cup cooked brown rice

In a saucepan, bring juice to a gentle boil. Add mix-and-water combination and rice. Stir constantly for 3 minutes until soup thickens. Serve alone or topped with thin orange slices or grated apple.

NUTTY SWEET AND SOUR SAUCE *(Makes 1 cup)*

Preparation and Cooking Time: 5 minutes

1 cup water

5 tablespoons Nut and Raisin Soup Mix dissolved in 1 tablespoon fresh lemon juice and 2 tablespoons water

In a saucepan, bring water to a boil. Add mix-water-and-juice combination. Stir constantly for 3 minutes until sauce thickens. May be used as a topping for grains or vegetables.

SWEET AND SOUR TOMATO SAUCE *(Makes 1¼ cups)*

Preparation and Cooking Time: 5 minutes

1 cup tomato juice

5 tablespoons Nut and Raisin Soup Mix dissolved in 4 tablespoons tomato juice

In a saucepan, bring juice to a gentle boil. Add mix-and-juice combination. Stir constantly for 3 minutes until sauce thickens. May be used over grain or vegetables.

CHAPTER FOUR

Salad Dressings and Dip Mixes

A dressing transforms a plate of vegetables into a delicious lunch or an appetizing side dish. Similarly, a dip changes a bowl of crackers or vegetable sticks into hors d'oeuvres or a midday snack.

Because the dressing is most responsible for the success of a salad, having several varieties of homemade dressing mixes on hand will ensure that salads are eaten eagerly. Most of the homemade dressing mixes in this chapter double as dips, which can be served with carrots, celery sticks, cauliflower, broccoli or as toppings for baked potatoes as well as with crackers or chips.

BASIC PARMESAN CHEESE MIX
(Makes nearly 1 cup mix)

¾ cup dried Parmesan cheese   ½ teaspoon oregano
½ teaspoon garlic powder   1½ teaspoons salt (optional)
¼ teaspoon black pepper   ½ teaspoon ground mustard

In a bowl, combine all ingredients and mix thoroughly. Spoon into a 1-cup wide-mouth jar, seal tightly and store in cool dry cupboard. Use within two months.

TOMATO CHEESE SALAD DRESSING (Makes ½ cup)

Preparation Time: 3 minutes

1 tablespoon Parmesan Cheese   3 tablespoons tomato juice
Mix   5 tablespoons olive oil

Place all ingredients in a jar, an electric blender or food processor and mix until well combined. May be used on vegetable salads or vegetable gelatin dishes.

VINEGAR CHEESE DRESSING (Makes ½ cup)

Preparation Time: 3 minutes

1 tablespoon Parmesan   1½ tablespoons cider vinegar
Cheese Mix   6½ tablespoons olive oil

Place all ingredients in a jar, an electric blender or food processor, and mix until well combined. May be used on vegetable salads.

PARMESAN SOY DRESSING (Makes ½ cup)

Preparation Time: 3 minutes

1 tablespoon Parmesan Cheese Mix	1 tablespoon tamari soy sauce
	7 tablespoons olive oil

Place all ingredients in a jar, an electric blender or food processor and mix until well combined. May be used on vegetable salads of all kinds.

SWEET AND SOUR PARMESAN CHEESE DRESSING (Makes ½ cup)

Preparation Time: 3 minutes

1 tablespoon Parmesan Cheese Mix	1 tablespoon cider vinegar
	1 tablespoon honey
	6 tablespoons sesame oil

Place all ingredients in a jar, an electric blender or food processor and mix until well combined. May be used on any vegetable salad.

SOUR CREAM PARMESAN DIP (Makes ½ cup)

Preparation Time: 3 minutes

1 tablespoon Parmesan Cheese Mix	½ cup sour cream

In a small bowl or food processor combine mix and sour cream. The flavor of this dip will increase if allowed to stand for an hour before serving. Serve with cut-up raw vegetables, potato chips or crackers.

YOGURT PARMESAN DIP (*Makes ½ cup*)

Preparation Time: 3 minutes

1 tablespoon Parmesan
Cheese Mix

½ teaspoon tomato paste
½ cup yogurt

In a small bowl or food processor combine mix, tomato paste and yogurt. The dip will become more flavorful if allowed to stand for an hour. Serve with cut-up raw vegetables, potato chips or crackers.

BASIC FRENCH DRESSING MIX
(*Makes ¾ cup mix*)

3 tablespoons ground
mustard
3 tablespoons paprika

2 tablespoons garlic powder
2½ tablespoons salt or salt
substitute
1½ tablespoons black pepper

In a small bowl, combine all ingredients and mix thoroughly. Spoon into a wide-mouth jar, seal tightly and store in a cool dark cupboard. Use within three months.

FRENCH DRESSING (*Makes ½ cup*)

Preparation Time: 3 minutes

1 teaspoon French Dressing
Mix

3 tablespoons lemon juice
5 tablespoons olive oil

Place all ingredients in a jar, an electric blender or food processor and mix until well combined. Serve on tossed salads.

FRENCH FRUIT DRESSING (*Makes ½ cup*)

Preparation Time: 3 minutes

1 teaspoon French Dressing Mix	4 tablespoons orange juice 4 tablespoons safflower oil

Place all ingredients in a jar, an electric blender or food processor and mix until well combined. May be used on vegetable salads, grated apple salad or mixed fruit and nut salad.

CREAM CHEESE FRENCH DRESSING (*Makes ½ cup*)

Preparation Time: 3 minutes

1 teaspoon French Dressing Mix	1 tablespoon cider vinegar 2 tablespoons cream cheese
	5 tablespoons olive oil

Blend all ingredients until smooth in an electric blender or food processor. May be used on vegetable salads.

FRENCH TOMATO DRESSING (*Makes ½ cup*)

Preparation Time: 3 minutes

1 teaspoon French Dressing Mix	2 tablespoons tomato juice 1 tablespoon lemon juice
	5 tablespoons olive oil

Place all ingredients in a jar, an electric blender or food processor and mix until well combined. May be used on any vegetable tossed salad.

SOUR CREAM FRENCH DRESSING (Makes ½ cup)

Preparation Time: 3 minutes

1 teaspoon French Dressing   2 tablespoons sour cream
  Mix   1 tablespoon cider vinegar
                    5 tablespoons olive oil

In a small bowl or food processor mix all ingredients until well combined. Serve with any vegetable tossed salad.

AVOCADO DRESSING (Makes ½ cup)

Preparation Time: 4 minutes

1 teaspoon French Dressing   1 tablespoon lemon juice
  Mix   3 tablespoons olive oil
                    ½ ripe avocado

Blend all ingredients in an electric blender or food processor until smooth. May be used on any vegetable or tossed salad.

RAVIGOTE DRESSING (Makes ½ cup)

Preparation Time: 3 minutes

1 teaspoon French Dressing   ½ teaspoon chopped parsley
  Mix   2 tablespoons lemon juice
1 tablespoon chopped onion   5 tablespoons olive oil

Place all ingredients in a jar, an electric blender or food processor and mix until combined. May be used on any vegetable or tossed salad.

BEET DRESSING (Makes ½ cup)

Preparation Time: 5 minutes

1 teaspoon French Dressing Mix	2 tablespoons lemon juice
	4 tablespoons olive oil
3 tablespoons cooked grated beets	

Blend all ingredients in an electric blender or food processor until smooth. May be used on vegetable salads or vegetable gelatin salads.

BLUE CHEESE DRESSING (Makes ½ cup)

Preparation Time: 3 minutes

1 teaspoon French Dressing Mix	4 tablespoons olive oil
	2 tablespoons crumbled blue cheese
2 tablespoons lemon juice	

Place all ingredients in a jar, an electric blender or food processor and mix until well combined. May be used on any tossed salad.

HORSERADISH DRESSING (Makes ½ cup)

Preparation Time: 3 minutes

1 teaspoon French Dressing Mix	2 tablespoons lemon juice
	4½ tablespoons olive oil
	1 teaspoon horseradish

Place all ingredients in a jar, an electric blender or food processor and mix until well combined. Can be served with any tossed vegetable salad.

BASIC HERB DRESSING MIX
(Makes 1 cup mix)

2 tablespoons dill seed	3 tablespoons dried chives
2 tablespoons tarragon	3 tablespoons dried parsley
1 tablespoon crushed rosemary	3 tablespoons nutritional yeast

1 tablespoon salt (optional)

In a small bowl, combine all ingredients until well distributed. Spoon into a wide-mouth jar, seal tightly and store in cool dark cupboard. Will remain fresh for two months.

HERB DRESSING *(Makes ½ cup)*

Preparation Time: 12 minutes

1 teaspoon Herb Dressing Mix	2 tablespoons lemon juice

5 tablespoons olive oil

Place ingredients in a jar and shake until well combined. Allow to stand for 10 minutes before serving. May be used on any tossed vegetable salad.

HERB CREAM DRESSING *(Makes ½ cup)*

Preparation Time: 10 minutes

1 teaspoon Herb Dressing Mix	1 tablespoon olive oil
1 tablespoon lemon juice	1 tablespoon water

5 tablespoons sour cream

In a small bowl, mix ingredients thoroughly. Allow to stand for 5 minutes before serving with any vegetable salad.

HERB TOMATO DRESSING (*Makes ½ cup*)

Preparation Time: 10 minutes

1 teaspoon Herb Dressing Mix   3 tablespoons tomato juice
5 tablespoons olive oil

Place all ingredients in a jar and shake well until thoroughly combined. Allow to stand for 5 minutes before serving. May be used on any vegetable tossed salad, grated carrot salad or cucumber salad.

BUTTERMILK HERB DRESSING (*Makes ½ cup*)

Preparation Time: 10 minutes

1 teaspoon Herb Dressing Mix   2 tablespoons olive oil
6 tablespoons buttermilk

Place all ingredients in a jar and shake well until thoroughly combined. Allow to stand for 5 minutes before serving. May be used on any vegetable or tossed salad.

HERB TOMATO CREAM DRESSING (*Makes ½ cup*)

Preparation Time: 10 minutes

1 teaspoon Herb Dressing Mix   4 tablespoons tomato juice
4 tablespoons sour cream

In a small bowl, mix all ingredients thoroughly. Allow to stand for 5 minutes before serving. May be used on any vegetable or tossed salad.

HERB TAHINI DRESSING (*Makes ½ cup*)

Preparation Time: 10 minutes

1 teaspoon Herb Dressing Mix   2 tablespoons lemon juice
3 tablespoons tahini   3 tablespoons water

In a small bowl, combine all ingredients until smooth. Allow to stand for 5 minutes before serving. May be used on tossed salad, as a dip for raw cut-up vegetables or as a sauce for cooked grain.

HERB SOUR CREAM DIP (*Makes ½ cup*)

Preparation Time: 10 minutes

1 teaspoon Herb Dressing   ½ cup sour cream
Mix

In a bowl, combine mix and sour cream. Allow to stand for 5 minutes before serving. Serve with raw cut-up vegetables, chips, crackers or as a topping for baked potatoes.

BASIC ITALIAN GARLIC DRESSING MIX
(*Makes ¾ cup mix*)

3 tablespoons garlic powder   2 tablespoons oregano
2 tablespoons dried minced   1 teaspoon black pepper
  onion   2 teaspoons paprika
2 teaspoons crumbled   ½ teaspoon ground allspice
  rosemary   1 tablespoon salt (optional)

In a small bowl, combine all ingredients and mix thoroughly. Spoon into a wide-mouth jar, seal tightly and store in cool dark cupboard. Will stay fresh for two months.

ITALIAN DRESSING (Makes ½ cup)

Preparation Time: 12 minutes

1½ teaspoons Italian Garlic   2 tablespoons cider vinegar
Dressing Mix   6 tablespoons olive oil

Place all ingredients in a jar and shake until well combined. Allow to stand for 10 minutes before serving. May be used on tossed green or mixed vegetable salads.

CREAMY ITALIAN DRESSING (Makes ½ cup)

Preparation Time: 10 minutes

1½ teaspoons Italian Garlic   2 tablespoons lemon juice
Dressing Mix   2 tablespoons olive oil
            4 tablespoons sour cream

In a small bowl, beat all ingredients until well combined and creamy. Allow to stand for 5 minutes before serving. May be used on any vegetable or tossed salad.

TAMARI GARLIC DRESSING (Makes ½ cup)

Preparation Time: 10 minutes

1½ teaspoons Italian Garlic   1 tablespoon tamari soy
Dressing Mix   sauce
        6 tablespoons sesame oil or olive oil

Place all ingredients in a jar and shake until well combined. Allow to stand for 5 minutes before serving. May be used on any vegetable or tossed salad.

GARLIC SOUR CREAM SAUCE (Makes ½ cup)

Preparation Time: 10 minutes

1½ teaspoons Italian Garlic
Dressing Mix

½ cup sour cream

In a small bowl, combine mix and sour cream. Allow to stand for 5 minutes before serving. Serve as a dip for chips, raw vegetables or crackers. It can also be used as a sauce for baked potatoes, steamed broccoli or asparagus.

ITALIAN TOMATO DRESSING (Makes ½ cup)

Preparation Time: 10 minutes

1½ teaspoons Italian Garlic
Dressing Mix

3 tablespoons tomato juice
5 tablespoons olive oil

Place all ingredients in a jar and shake until well combined. Allow to stand for 5 minutes before serving. Shake again just before using on any vegetable or tossed salad.

COTTAGE CHEESE DIP OR SAUCE (Makes ½ cup)

1½ teaspoons Italian Garlic
Dressing Mix
2 tablespoons water

6 tablespoons cottage
cheese

Blend ingredients in an electric blender or food processor until smooth. Allow to stand for 5 minutes before serving. Serve with raw vegetables, chips or crackers, or as a sauce for baked potatoes, steamed broccoli or asparagus.

GARLIC TOFU DIP (Makes ½ cup)

Preparation Time: 10 minutes

1½ teaspoons Italian Garlic
Dressing

3 tablespoons tomato juice
5 tablespoons tofu

Blend all ingredients in an electric blender or food processor until smooth. Allow to stand for 5 minutes before serving. Serve with raw vegetables, chips or crackers. It can also be used as a topping for baked potatoes.

BASIC SPICY MEXICAN DRESSING OR SAUCE MIX
(Makes ¾ cup mix)

3 tablespoons chili powder
3 tablespoons dried minced garlic
3 tablespoons dried minced onion

1 tablespoon salt (optional)
1 tablespoon ground cumin
1 teaspoon crumbled dried red chilies

In a small bowl, combine all ingredients and mix thoroughly. Spoon into a wide-mouth jar, seal tightly and store in cool dark cupboard. Will remain fresh for two months.

SPICY MEXICAN DRESSING (Makes ½ cup)

Preparation Time: 10 minutes

½ teaspoon Spicy Mexican
Dressing or Sauce Mix

3 tablespoons tomato juice
5 tablespoons olive oil

Place all ingredients in a jar and shake until well combined. Allow to stand for 5 minutes. Shake once again before serving. May be used on any vegetable or tossed vegetable salad.

TACO SAUCE (*Makes ½ cup*)

Preparation Time: 10 minutes

2 teaspoons Spicy Mexican
Dressing or Sauce Mix
½ cup tomato juice

1 teaspoon arrowroot starch
dissolved in 2 teaspoons
water

In a saucepan, combine mix and juice. Heat nearly to boiling. Stir in starch-and-water paste. Continue stirring constantly for 3 minutes until sauce thickens. May be used on tacos or tostadas.

MEXICAN SOUR CREAM DIP (*Makes ½ cup*)

Preparation Time: 7 minutes

1½ teaspoons Spicy Mexican
Dressing or Sauce Mix

½ cup sour cream

In a small bowl, beat together mix and sour cream. Allow to stand for 5 minutes before serving with raw cut-up vegetables, corn chips or crackers.

GUACAMOLE (*Makes ½ cup*)

Preparation Time: 5 minutes

2 teaspoons Spicy Mexican
Dressing or Sauce Mix

¼ cup sour cream
½ ripe avocado, mashed

In a small bowl, mix all ingredients until smooth. Serve with tortilla chips or on salads or tacos.

CREAMY MEXICAN SALAD DRESSING (Makes ½ cup)

Preparation Time: 3 minutes

1½ teaspoons Spicy Mexican Dressing or Sauce Mix	¼ cup sour cream ¼ cup olive oil

In a small bowl, beat ingredients with a wire whisk until smooth and creamy. May be used on any vegetable or vegetable tossed salad.

BASIC CURRIED DRESSING MIX
(*Makes ¾ cup mix*)

3 tablespoons ground cumin	1 tablespoon ground cardamom
3 tablespoons ground coriander	1 tablespoon ground ginger
1 tablespoon black pepper	1 teaspoon cayenne
1 tablespoon turmeric	1 teaspoon salt (optional)
1 tablespoon ground cinnamon	1 teaspoon mustard seed

In a small bowl, combine all ingredients and mix thoroughly. Spoon into a wide-mouth jar, seal tightly and store in cool dark cupboard. Will stay fresh for two months.

CURRIED DRESSING (Makes ½ cup)

Preparation Time: 5 minutes

2 teaspoons Curried Dressing Mix	2½ tablespoons lemon juice 5½ tablespoons olive oil

Place all ingredients in a jar, an electric blender or food processor and mix until well combined. May be used on any vegetable or tossed salad.

CURRIED TOMATO DRESSING (Makes ½ cup)

Preparation Time: 5 minutes

2 teaspoons Curried Dressing   3 tablespoons tomato juice
Mix   5 tablespoons olive oil

Place all ingredients in a jar, an electric blender or food processor and mix until well combined. May be used on any vegetable or as salad dressing.

CURRY DIP (Makes ½ cup)

Preparation Time: 5 minutes

2 teaspoons Curried Dressing   ½ cup sour cream
Mix

In a bowl or food processor mix ingredients until well combined. May be served with chips, crackers or raw cut-up vegetables or it may be used as a topping for baked potatoes, steamed broccoli or asparagus.

CURRY CREAM DRESSING (Makes ½ cup)

Preparation Time: 5 minutes

2 teaspoons Curried Dressing   1 tablespoon lemon juice
Mix   3 tablespoons olive oil
              4 tablespoons sour cream

In a small bowl or food processor mix ingredients until smooth and creamy. May be used on cooked vegetables or salad.

RAITA (*Makes ½ cup*)

Preparation Time: 5 minutes

2 teaspoons Curried Dressing   3 tablespoons grated
    Mix   cucumber
½ cup yogurt

In a small bowl, beat mix and yogurt with a whisk. Stir in cucumber and serve as a side dish with an Indian meal.

CURRIED FRUIT DRESSING (*Makes ½ cup*)

Preparation Time: 5 minutes

2 teaspoons Curried Dressing   2 tablespoons crushed
    Mix   pineapple, unsweetened
       6 tablespoons sour cream

In a small bowl, mix all ingredients. May be used on fruit salad or as a topping for fresh pineapple or papayas.

CHAPTER FIVE

Hearty Bean Mixes for Stews, Casseroles and Main Dishes

In many traditional cultures high protein legumes are a staple. In India, many kinds of beans and peas are curried; in the Middle East, chick-peas are pureed to make humous; in Mexico, pinto beans are used in tostadas, burritos, tacos, enchiladas and chili; and in Europe, lentils are a favorite soup ingredient.

Unfortunately, here in North America, where a large variety of beans and peas grow plentifully, they are often overlooked in favor of foods quicker to prepare, but much more expensive. Yet even the busiest cook can work these inexpensive, high protein staples into the family diet via the mix-ahead system.

The easiest way for a cook who works outside the home to prepare beans is with the help of an electric crock pot (slow cooker). In this book we show how bean mixes can be put on in the morning and eaten within 15 minutes of arriving home in the evening. With very little extra time or bother these same beans can be made into a variety of casseroles.

For others, to whom cooking beans in a pot or pressure cooker is more convenient, we have provided a different method of cooking and spicing the same mixes.

Each utensil requires a different amount of liquid as well as a varied method of spicing. Therefore, we have provided separate directions for each bean dish depending on the utensil used to cook the recipe.

The soaking stage of preparation has been eliminated in the preparation of bean mixes. Although most recipes call for soaking, a good deal of controversy continues over the necessity of doing so. Some people even report that beans are more easily digested when they are not presoaked. We have eliminated the soaking as a time-saving measure. But it is important to remember that whatever the method of cooking beans, it is essential that they be well cooked if they are to be easily digested. Beans should be soft, with no remaining taste of starch, for maximum flavor and usable nutrition.

BASIC SOUTHERN BLACK-EYED PEA MIX
(Makes five 12-ounce jars)

5 cups black-eyed peas	5 teaspoons dried minced
⅔ cup dried minced onion	garlic
⅓ cup dried parsley	2½ teaspoons black pepper
1 tablespoon dried chives	1 tablespoon salt (optional)

Measure 1 cup beans into each of 5 wide-mouth jars. In a small bowl, combine remaining ingredients and mix thoroughly. Spoon ¼ cup of this mixture into 5 small plastic bags. Place 1 bag in each jar. Seal jars tightly and store in cool dark cupboard. Use within two months for maximum flavor.

SOUTHERN HOPPING JOHN *(Serves 4)*

Preparation Time in a Crock Pot: 8 to 10 hours

1 jar Southern Black-Eyed Pea Mix	3⅔ cups water

Remove seasoning and place in ⅓ cup water. Set aside. In a crock pot, combine remaining 3⅓ cups water with peas. Cook on high for 8 to 10 hours while at work or overnight. Stir in seasoning in water 15 minutes before serving.

Preparation Time in a Pot: 2½ hours

1 jar Southern Black-Eyed   3¾ cups water
  Pea Mix

Remove seasoning and set aside.
Place peas and water in a covered pot. Bring to a boil for 10 minutes. Reduce heat to medium low and cook for 2 hours until beans are soft. Stir in seasoning and cook for 20 minutes, until onions are tender, before serving.

Preparation Time in a Pressure Cooker: 1½ hours

1 jar Southern Black-Eyed   3 cups water
  Pea Mix

Place seasoning mixture, peas and water in a pressure cooker. Cover and cook on high until pressure reaches 15 pounds. Reduce heat to low and cook for 1¼ hours. Decrease pressure according to manufacturer's instructions.

BLACK-EYED PEA PIE (*Makes one 9-inch pie*)

Preparation Time: 10 minutes
Baking Time: 35 minutes

1 recipe Southern Hopping   ¼ cup soft butter
  John (previous recipe)   1 tablespoon water
1 cup cornmeal   ⅔ cup grated Cheddar cheese

Preheat oven to 400 degrees.
Stir Southern Hopping John vigorously until mixture becomes creamy. Set aside. In a bowl, blend cornmeal and butter with fingers until cornmeal is thoroughly coated. Stir

in water until mixture is moistened. Press mixture into a 9-inch pie plate. Pour in Southern Hopping John. Sprinkle with cheese and bake for 35 minutes until crust is golden brown.

BLACK-EYED PEA STUFFED PEPPERS (Serves 4 to 6)

Preparation Time: 10 minutes
Baking Time: 25 minutes

1 recipe Southern Hopping John (p. 76)
1 cup cooked rice
8 green peppers

2 tablespoons oil
4 tablespoons chopped sweet red peppers

In a bowl, mix Southern Hopping John and cooked rice. Stem and seed green peppers, leaving shells intact. Spoon black-eyed pea mixture into green peppers. Rub oil on the outside of each pepper. Place upright in a casserole or baking dish. Bake at 350 degrees for 25 minutes. Remove from oven and garnish top opening of each stuffed pepper with ½ tablespoon chopped sweet red pepper.

BLACK-EYED PEA AND CORN COBBLER
(Serves 4 to 6)

Preparation Time: 15 minutes
Baking Time: 25 minutes

1 recipe Southern Hopping John (p. 76)
2 cups corn kernels

½ recipe Cornbread (p. 67), unbaked
1 tablespoon melted butter

Preheat oven to 375 degrees.

In a bowl, mix Southern Hopping John and corn kernels. Turn into an oiled casserole dish. Spoon cornbread batter over beans. Sprinkle with melted butter and bake for 25 minutes until top is golden brown.

BLACK-EYED PEA AND TOMATO DINNER
(Serves 4 to 6)

Preparation Time in a Crock Pot: 8 to 10 hours

1 jar Southern Black-Eyed Pea Mix	3⅔ cups water 6 whole tomatoes, peeled
	1 tablespoon tomato paste

Remove seasoning mixture and place in ⅓ cup water. Set aside. In crock pot combine peas, tomatoes and remaining 3⅓ cups water. Cook on high for 8 to 10 hours. Stir in seasoning in water and add tomato paste before serving.

Preparation Time in a Pot: 3 hours

1 jar Southern Black-Eyed Pea Mix	3½ cups water 6 whole tomatoes, peeled
	1 tablespoon tomato paste

Remove seasoning mixture and set aside.

In a covered pot combine peas and water. Boil for 10 minutes and reduce heat to medium low.

Add whole tomatoes and cook for 2½ hours until peas are soft. Stir in seasoning and tomato paste and cook for 20 minutes before serving.

Preparation Time in a Pressure Cooker: 1½ hours

1 jar Southern Black-Eyed Pea Mix	3 cups water 6 whole tomatoes, peeled
	1 tablespoon tomato paste

Place pea mix with seasoning, water and tomatoes in a pressure cooker. Cover and cook on high heat until pressure reaches 15 pounds. Reduce heat to low and cook for 1¼ hours. Reduce pressure according to manufacturer's instructions.

Stir in tomato paste just before serving.

BASIC BOSTON BEAN MIX
(Makes five 12-ounce jars)

5 cups navy beans	1 tablespoon garlic powder
1¼ cups date sugar	½ teaspoon cayenne
3 tablespoons ground	(optional)
mustard	2½ teaspoons salt (optional)

Measure 1 cup beans into each of 5 wide-mouth jars. Add ¼ cup date sugar directly to each jar. In a small bowl, mix together remaining ingredients. Spoon 1 tablespoon of mixture directly into each jar. Seal jars tightly and store in cool dry cupboard. Use within four months.

BOSTON BEANS (Serves 4)

Preparation Time in a Crock Pot: 8 to 10 hours

1 jar Boston Bean Mix	3 cups water

In a crock pot, combine mix and water. Set on high and cook for 8 to 10 hours while at work or overnight.

Preparation Time in a Pot: 3 hours

1 jar Boston Bean Mix	3¼ cups water

In a covered pot, combine bean mix and water. Bring to a boil and reduce heat to medium low. Cook for 3 hours until beans are soft.

Preparation Time in a Pressure Cooker: 1½ hours

1 jar Boston Bean Mix	2¾ cups water

Place bean mix and water in a pressure cooker. Cover and cook on high heat until pressure is increased to 15 pounds. Reduce heat to low and cook for 1 hour and 20 minutes. Decrease pressure according to manufacturer's instructions.

Preparation Time in an Oven: 6 hours

1 jar Boston Bean Mix   3 cups water

Combine bean mix and water in a casserole and bake, covered, at 325 degrees for 6 hours, until beans are soft.

NAVY BEAN STUFFED ACORN SQUASH
(*Serves 4 to 6*)

Preparation Time: 5 minutes
Baking Time: 40 minutes

3 acorn squash   1 recipe Boston Beans (p. 80)

Divide each squash in two and remove seeds and pulp. Spoon beans into squash and bake upright in casserole at 400 degrees for 40 minutes until soft.

BOSTON BEAN TURNOVERS (*Serves 4*)

Preparation Time: 15 minutes
Baking Time: 30 minutes

1 double recipe Rolled Pie   1 recipe Boston Beans (p. 80)
  Crust (p. 206)   2 tablespoons melted butter

Roll out pie dough and cut into 6-inch squares. Place 3 tablespoons beans in the center of each square. Fold over dough to form triangles, press seams closed with a fork and prick the tops with fork.

Place on a well-oiled baking sheet and bake for 30 minutes until lightly browned.

BOSTON BEANS WITH FRUIT (Serves 4 to 6)

Preparation Time in a Crock Pot: 8 to 10 hours

1 jar Boston Bean Mix	½ cup raisins or currants
3¼ cups water	½ cup dried pears
1 apple or pear, peeled, sliced	½ cup dried apricots

Place all ingredients in a crock pot and set on high. Cook covered for 8 to 10 hours and serve at once.

Preparation Time in a Pot: 3 hours

1 jar Boston Bean Mix	½ cup raisins or currants
3½ cups water	½ cup dried pears
2 apples or pears, peeled, sliced	½ cup dried apricots

Place bean mix in a covered pot. Bring to a boil. Reduce heat to medium low and add remaining ingredients.

Cook covered, stirring occasionally, for 2½ to 3 hours, until beans are soft.

Preparation Time in a Pressure Cooker: 1½ hours

1 jar Boston Bean Mix	½ cup raisins or currants
3 cups water	½ cup dried pears
1 apple or pear, peeled, sliced	½ cup dried apricots

Place all ingredients in pressure cooker. Cook on high until pressure reaches 15 pounds. Reduce heat to low and cook for 1¼ hours. Reduce pressure according to manufacturer's instructions.

SWEET AND SOUR BEAN STEW (Serves 4)

Preparation Time in a Crock Pot: 8 to 10 hours

1 jar Boston Bean Mix
3½ cups water
2 carrots, cut in 1-inch
  chunks

6 small onions, peeled
6 whole baby potatoes
2 tablespoons tomato paste
1 teaspoon cider vinegar

Combine bean mix, water, carrots, onions and potatoes in crock pot. Set on high and cook covered for 8 to 10 hours while at work or overnight.

Stir in tomato paste and cider vinegar and cook for 5 minutes before serving.

Preparation Time in a Pot: 3 hours

1 jar Boston Bean Mix
3¾ cups water
2 carrots, cut in 1-inch
  chunks
6 small onions, peeled

6 whole baby potatoes
2 tablespoons tomato paste
1 teaspoon apple cider
  vinegar

Place bean mix and water in a pot. Bring to a boil. Reduce heat to medium low and add carrots, onions and potatoes. Cover and cook for 2½ to 3 hours until beans are soft.

Stir in tomato paste and vinegar and cook for 5 minutes before serving.

Preparation Time in a Pressure Cooker: 1½ hours

1 jar Boston Bean Mix
3¼ cups water
2 carrots, cut in 1-inch
  chunks
6 small onions, peeled

6 whole baby potatoes
2 tablespoons tomato paste
1 teaspoon apple cider
  vinegar

Place all ingredients in a pressure cooker. Cover and cook on high until pressure increases to 15 pounds. Reduce heat to medium low and cook for 1¼ hours. Decrease pressure according to manufacturer's instructions.

BASIC DARK VARIETY BEAN MIX*
(Makes five 12-ounce jars; each jar serves 4)

1 cup pinto beans	5 teaspoons dried parsley
1 cup kidney beans	5 teaspoons ground cumin
1 cup black beans	2½ teaspoons basil
1 cup aduki beans	5 bay leaves
1 cup mung beans	5 tablespoons dried minced
5 tablespoons dried minced	onion
garlic	

Mix beans well and measure 1 cup bean mix into each of
the 5 wide-mouth jars. In a small bowl, combine remaining
ingredients and mix thoroughly. Spoon 2 tablespoons plus 1
teaspoon of this seasoning mixture and 1 bay leaf into each of
5 plastic bags and place 1 bag in each jar. Seal jars tightly
and store in cool dark cupboard. Use within two months.

THICK BEAN STEW (Serves 4)

Preparation Time in a Crock Pot: 8 to 10 hours

1 jar Dark Variety Bean Mix   4 cups water

Remove bag of seasoning and pour into ½ cup water. Set
aside.

Pour rest of water and beans in a slow cooker and cook,
covered, for 8 to 10 hours. Stir in seasoning in water 15 minutes before serving.

Preparation Time in a Pot: 4 to 5 hours

1 jar Dark Variety Bean Mix   4 cups water

Remove bag of seasoning and set aside. Pour mix and
water into a pot, and then boil for 10 minutes. Reduce heat
to medium low; add seasoning mixture and cook, covered, for
4 to 5 hours, until beans are soft.

---

* The black beans in this mix will clog the vent of a pressure cooker.

VARIETY BEAN AND VEGETABLE POT (Serves 4)

Preparation Time in a Crock Pot: 8 to 10 hours

1 jar Dark Variety Bean Mix   1½ cups root vegetables in
4½ cups water   2-inch chunks (potatoes,
                                                yams, carrots, onions,
                                                turnips and/or parsnips)

Remove seasoning and place in ½ cup water. Set aside.
Place beans, water and vegetables in a slow cooker. Set on
high and cook for 8 to 10 hours. Stir in seasoning in water 15
minutes before serving.

Preparation Time in a Pot: 4 to 5 hours

1 jar Dark Variety Bean Mix   1½ cups root vegetables in
5 cups water   2-inch chunks (potatoes,
                                                yams, carrots, onions,
                                                turnips and/or parsnips)

Remove bag of seasoning and set aside.
Place beans and water in a pot and boil for 10 minutes.
Reduce heat to medium low. Add vegetables and seasoning
mixture, and continue cooking until beans are soft.

BEANS IN TOMATO SAUCE (Serves 4)

Preparation Time in a Crock Pot: 8 to 10 hours

1 jar Dark Variety Bean Mix   4 cups water
            2 tablespoons tomato paste

Remove bag of seasoning and place in ½ cup water. Set
aside.
Place beans and rest of water in an electric crock pot. Set
on high. Cook, covered, for 8 to 10 hours overnight or while
at work. Stir in tomato paste and seasoning in water 15 minutes before serving.

Preparation Time in a Pot: 4 to 6 hours

1 jar Dark Variety Bean Mix   5½ cups water
            2 tablespoons tomato paste

Remove seasoning and set aside.
Place beans and water in a pot. Boil for 10 minutes. Reduce heat to medium low and add seasoning. Cook until beans are tender. Stir in tomato paste before serving.

DARK VARIETY BEAN AND WHEAT STEW
(*Serves 4*)

Preparation Time in a Crock Pot: 8 to 10 hours

1 jar Dark Variety Bean Mix   1 cup whole wheat berries
            6 cups water

Remove seasoning and place in ½ cup water. Set aside.
Place beans, wheat berries and rest of water in a slow cooker. Set on high and cook for 8 to 10 hours overnight or while at work. Stir in seasoning in water 15 minutes before serving.

Preparation Time in a Pot: 4 to 6 hours

1 jar Dark Variety Bean Mix   1 cup whole wheat berries
            7½ cups water

Remove seasoning and set aside.
In a covered pot boil beans, wheat and water for 10 minutes. Reduce heat to medium low. Stir in seasoning and cook 4 to 6 hours until beans are soft.

DARK VARIETY BEAN SALAD (*Serves 4*)

Preparation Time in a Crock Pot: 8 to 10 hours

    1 jar Dark Variety Bean Mix   2 teaspoons cider vinegar
3½ cups water   3 tablespoons olive oil

Remove seasoning and place in ½ cup water. Set aside.
Place beans and water in crock pot. Set on high and cook, covered, overnight or while at work. Add seasoning in water and cook for 15 minutes. Allow beans to cool and toss with vinegar and oil.

Preparation Time in a Pot: 4 to 6 hours

1 jar Dark Variety Bean Mix	2 teaspoons cider vinegar
4 cups water	3 tablespoons olive oil

Remove seasoning and set aside.
Place beans and water in a covered pot. Boil for 10 minutes. Reduce heat to medium low and add seasoning. Cook 4 to 6 hours until soft. Place cooked beans in a bowl, and refrigerate until cool. Toss with cider vinegar and olive oil.

BASIC SPLIT GREEN PEA MIX
(*Makes five 12-ounce jars; each jar serves 4*)

5 cups split green peas	2 teaspoons celery seed
⅓ cup dried minced onion	2 tablespoons dried parsley
2 teaspoons dried minced garlic	2 teaspoons basil
	2 teaspoons tarragon

1 teaspoon thyme

Measure 1 cup peas into each of 5 wide-mouth jars. In a small bowl, combine remaining ingredients and mix thoroughly. Spoon 3½ teaspoons of this seasoning mixture into 5 small plastic bags and place 1 bag in each jar. Seal jars tightly and store in cool dark cupboard. Use within two months.

HEARTY GREEN PEA SOUP (Serves 4)

Preparation Time in a Crock Pot: 8 to 10 hours

1 jar Split Green Pea Mix   3 cups water

Remove seasoning and place in ¼ cup water. Set aside. Place peas and remaining 2¾ cups water in an electric crock pot. Set on high and cook, covered, for 8 to 10 hours while at work or overnight. Stir in seasoning in water. Cook for 15 minutes.

Preparation Time in a Pot: 1½ hours

1 jar Split Green Pea Mix   3¼ cups water

Remove seasoning and set aside. Place peas and water in a covered pot. Boil for 10 minutes. Reduce heat to medium low. Stir in seasoning. Cook, covered, for 1¼ hours until soft.

Preparation Time in a Pressure Cooker: 45 minutes

1 jar Split Green Pea Mix   2½ cups water

Place seasoning mixture, peas and water in a pressure cooker. Cover and cook over high heat until pressure reaches 15 pounds. Reduce heat to low and cook for 45 minutes. Decrease pressure according to manufacturer's instructions.

GREEN PEA AND RICE STEW (Serves 4)

Preparation Time in a Crock Pot: 8 to 10 hours

1 jar Split Green Pea Mix   5 cups water
⅔ cup brown rice

Remove seasoning and place in ¼ cup water. Set aside. Place peas, rice and remaining water in an electric crock pot. Set on high and cook, covered, for 8 to 10 hours while at work or overnight. Stir in seasoning in water and cook for 15 minutes.

Preparation Time in a Pot: 1½ hours

1 jar Split Green Pea Mix   ¾ cup brown rice
                    5 cups water

Remove seasoning and set aside.
Place peas, rice and water in a covered pot. Boil for 10 minutes. Reduce heat to medium low. Stir in seasoning. Cook, covered, for 1¼ hours until soft.

Preparation Time in a Pressure Cooker: 45 minutes

1 jar Split Green Pea Mix   ⅔ cup brown rice
                    4 cups water

Place seasoning mixture, peas, rice and water in a pressure cooker. Cover and cook over high heat until pressure reaches 15 pounds. Reduce heat to low and cook for 45 minutes. Decrease pressure according to manufacturer's instructions.

GREEN PEA AND MILLET CASSEROLE (*Serves 4*)

Preparation Time in a Crock Pot: 8 to 10 hours

1 jar Split Green Pea Mix   1 cup millet
5 cups water   ⅔ cup grated Cheddar cheese

Remove seasoning and place in ¼ cup water. Set aside.
Place peas, millet and remaining 4¾ cups water in an electric crock pot. Set on high and cook, covered, for 8 to 10 hours while at work or overnight. Stir in seasoning in water. Cook for 15 minutes.
Pour into casserole dish. Sprinkle with cheese and place under broiler for five minutes until cheese has melted.

Preparation Time in a Pot: 1½ hours

1 jar Split Green Pea Mix	5 cups water
1 cup millet	⅔ cup grated Cheddar cheese

Remove seasoning and set aside.

Place peas, millet and water in a covered pot. Boil for 10 minutes. Reduce heat to medium low. Stir in seasoning. Cook, covered, for 1 hour until soft.

Turn into a casserole dish. Sprinkle with cheese. Place under a broiler for 5 minutes until cheese has melted.

Preparation Time in a Pressure Cooker: 45 minutes

1 jar Split Green Pea Mix	4½ cups water
1 cup millet	⅔ cup grated Cheddar cheese

Place seasoning mixture, peas, millet and water in a pressure cooker. Cover and cook over high heat until pressure reaches 15 pounds. Reduce heat to low and cook for 35 minutes.

Turn into casserole dish. Sprinkle with grated cheese and place under broiler until cheese has melted.

GREEN PEA AND VEGETABLE SOUP (*Serves 4*)

Preparation Time in a Crock Pot: 8 to 10 hours

1 jar Split Green Pea Mix	1½ cups diced root vegetables
4½ cups water	(carrots, parsnips, onions and/or yams)

Remove seasoning and place in ¼ cup water. Set aside.

Place peas, vegetables and remaining 4¼ cups water in an electric crock pot. Set on high and cook, covered, for 8 to 10 hours while at work or overnight. Stir in seasoning in water. Cook for 15 minutes before serving.

Preparation Time in a Pot: 1 hour

1 jar Split Green Pea Mix
5 cups water

1½ cups diced root vegetables
(carrots, parsnips, onions
and/or yams)

Remove seasoning and set aside.
Place peas and water in a covered pot. Boil for 10 minutes.
Reduce heat to medium low. Stir in seasoning and vegetables.
Cook, covered, for 50 minutes.

Preparation Time in a Pressure Cooker: 35 minutes

1 jar Split Green Pea Mix
4 cups water

1½ cups diced root vegetables
(carrots, parsnips, onions
and/or yams)

Place seasoning mixture, peas, vegetables and water in a
pressure cooker. Cover and cook over high heat until pressure reaches 15 pounds. Reduce heat to low and cook for 35
minutes. Decrease pressure according to manufacturer's instructions.

BASIC CURRIED CHICK-PEA MIX
(Makes five 12-ounce jars; each jar serves 4)

5 cups chick-peas
5 teaspoons mustard seed
⅔ cup dried minced onion
5 teaspoons turmeric
1¼ teaspoons cayenne
2½ teaspoons black pepper

2½ teaspoons ground
cinnamon
2½ teaspoons ground
cardamom
2½ teaspoons salt or salt
substitute

Measure 1 cup chick-peas into each of 5 wide-mouth jars.
In a small bowl, combine remaining ingredients and mix
thoroughly. Spoon 3½ tablespoons of this seasoning mixture
into 5 plastic bags and place 1 bag in each jar. Seal jars
tightly and store in cool dark cupboard.

CURRIED CHICK-PEAS (Serves 4)

Preparation Time in a Crock Pot: 8 to 10 hours

1 jar Curried Chick-Pea Mix   3½ cups water

Remove seasoning and place in ¼ cup water. Set aside.
Place beans and remaining 3¼ cups water in an electric crock pot. Set on high and cook, covered, for 8 to 10 hours while at work or overnight. Stir in seasoning in water. Cook for 15 minutes before serving.

Preparation Time in a Pot: 4 hours

1 jar Curried Chick-Pea Mix   4 cups water

Remove seasoning and set aside.
Place beans and water in a covered pot. Boil for 10 minutes. Reduce heat to medium low. Stir in seasoning. Cook, covered, for 4 hours until soft.

Preparation Time in a Pressure Cooker: 2 hours

1 jar Curried Chick-Pea Mix   2½ cups water

Place seasoning mixture, peas and water in a pressure cooker. Cover and cook over high heat until pressure reaches 15 pounds. Reduce heat to low and cook for 2 hours. Decrease pressure according to manufacturer's instructions.

CHICK-PEA CURRY WITH SOUR CREAM (Serves 4)

Preparation Time in a Crock Pot: 8 to 10 hours

1 jar Curried Chick-Pea Mix   3¾ cups water
1 cup sour cream

Remove seasoning and place in ¼ cup water. Set aside.
Place peas and remaining 3½ cups water in an electric crock pot. Set on high and cook, covered, for 8 to 10 hours

while at work or overnight. Stir in seasoning in water and sour cream. Cook for 15 minutes.

Preparation Time in a Pot: 4 hours

1 jar Curried Chick-Pea Mix   4½ cups water
1 cup sour cream

Remove seasoning and set aside.
Place peas and water in a covered pot. Boil for 10 minutes. Reduce heat to medium low. Stir in seasoning. Cook, covered, for 4 hours until soft. Stir in sour cream just before serving.

Preparation Time in a Pressure Cooker: 2 hours

1 jar Curried Chick-Pea Mix   2¾ cups water
1 cup sour cream

Place seasoning mixture, peas and water in a pressure cooker. Cover and cook over high heat until pressure reaches 15 pounds. Reduce heat to low and cook for 2 hours. Decrease pressure according to manufacturer's instructions.

CURRIED CHICK-PEAS IN TOMATO SAUCE
(Serves 4)

Preparation Time in a Crock Pot: 8 to 10 hours

1 jar Curried Chick-Pea Mix   4 cups water
3 tablespoons tomato paste

Remove seasoning and place in ¼ cup water. Set aside.
Place chick-peas and remaining 3¾ cups water in an electric crock pot. Set on high and cook, covered, for 8 to 10 hours while at work or overnight. Stir in seasoning in water and tomato paste. Cook for 15 minutes before serving.

Preparation Time in a Pot: 4 hours

1 jar Curried Chick-Pea Mix   4½ cups water
      3 tablespoons tomato paste

Remove seasoning and set aside.
Place chick-peas and water in a covered pot. Boil for 10 minutes. Reduce heat to medium low.
Cook for 3 hours until soft. Stir in seasoning and tomato paste and cook for 45 minutes before serving.

Preparation Time in a Pressure Cooker: 2 hours

1 jar Curried Chick-Pea Mix   3½ cups water
      3 tablespoons tomato paste

Place seasoning mixture, chick-peas and water in a pressure cooker. Cover and cook over high heat until pressure reaches 15 pounds. Reduce heat to low and cook for 2 hours. Decrease pressure according to manufacturer's instructions. Stir in tomato paste before serving.

CHICK-PEA STUFFED TOMATOES (*Serves 4*)

Preparation Time: 10 minutes
Baking Time: 20 minutes (optional)

4 large firm tomatoes   2 cups cooked Curried
                                       Chick-Peas in Tomato Sauce
                                       (previous recipe)
                   4 sprigs parsley

Slice off caps of tomatoes. With a grapefruit spoon remove seeds and pulp. Chop seeds and pulp fine and stir into curried chick-peas. Spoon mixture into hollowed tomatoes.
These stuffed tomatoes can be served immediately or baked for 20 minutes at 325 degrees. Garnish with parsley before serving.

CURRIED CHICK-PEA AND EGGPLANT CASSEROLE
(Serves 4 to 6)

Preparation Time: 5 minutes
Baking Time: 6 hours

1 jar Curried Chick-Pea Mix	2 cups peeled and diced
4 cups water	eggplant
½ cup sour cream or yogurt	

In a casserole, combine chick-pea mix and water. Bake, covered, in a 400 degree oven for 4 hours. Stir in eggplant and cook, uncovered, for 2 hours, until beans and eggplant are soft.

Top with sour cream or yogurt just before serving.

BASIC MIDDLE EAST STYLE CHICK-PEA MIX
(Makes five 12-ounce jars; each jar serves 4)

5 cups chick-peas	1 tablespoon ground
2 tablespoons dried minced	coriander
garlic	1¼ teaspoons cayenne
2 tablespoons ground cumin	1¼ teaspoons salt or salt
	substitute

Measure 1 cup chick-peas into each of 5 wide-mouth jars. In a small bowl, combine remaining ingredients and mix thoroughly. Spoon 1 tablespoon plus ½ teaspoon of this seasoning mixture into 5 small plastic bags and place 1 bag in each jar. Seal jars tightly and store in cool dark cupboard. Use within two months.

MIDDLE EAST CHICK-PEAS (Serves 4)

Preparation Time in a Crock Pot: 8 to 10 hours

1 jar Middle East Style	4 cups water
Chick-Pea Mix	

Remove seasoning and place in ¼ cup water. Set aside. Place chick-peas and remaining 3¾ cups water in an electric crock pot. Set on high and cook, covered, for 8 to 10 hours while at work or overnight. Stir in seasoning in water. Cook for 15 minutes. Remove ½ cup cooked chick-peas and mash. Stir back into chick-peas to form a sauce before serving.

Preparation Time in a Pot: 4½ hours

1 jar Middle East Style   4½ cups water
Chick-Pea Mix

Remove seasoning and set aside. Place chick-peas and water in a covered pot. Boil for 10 minutes. Reduce heat to medium low. Stir in seasoning. Cook, covered, for 4 hours, until soft. Remove ½ cup chick-peas and mash. Return to chick-peas in pot and stir to form sauce before serving.

Preparation Time in a Pressure Cooker: 2 hours

1 jar Middle East Style   3½ cups water
Chick-Pea Mix

Place seasoning mixture, chick-peas and water in a pressure cooker. Cover and cook over high heat until pressure reaches 15 pounds. Reduce heat to low and cook for 2 hours. Decrease pressure according to manufacturer's instructions.

CHICK-PEA YOGURT STEW (Serves 4)

Preparation Time in a Crock Pot: 8 to 10 hours

1 jar Middle East Style   3¾ cups water
Chick-Pea Mix   1 cup yogurt

Remove seasoning and place in ¼ cup water. Set aside. Place chick-peas and remaining water in an electric crock pot. Set on high and cook, covered, for 8 to 10 hours while at work or overnight. Stir in seasoning in water and yogurt. Cook for 15 minutes.

Preparation Time in a Pot: 4½ hours

| 1 jar Middle East Style | 4 cups water |
| Chick-Pea Mix | 1 cup yogurt |

Remove seasoning and set aside. Place chick-peas and water in a covered pot. Boil for 10 minutes. Reduce heat to medium low. Stir in seasoning. Cook, covered, for 4 hours until soft. Stir in yogurt and continue cooking until yogurt is heated.

Preparation Time in a Pressure Cooker: 2 hours 10 minutes

| 1 jar Middle East Style | 3 cups water |
| Chick-Pea Mix | 1 cup yogurt |

Place seasoning mixture, chick-peas and water in a pressure cooker. Cover and cook over high heat until pressure reaches 15 pounds. Reduce heat to low and cook for 2 hours. Decrease pressure according to manufacturer's instructions. Stir in yogurt before serving.

HUMOUS (MIDDLE EASTERN CHICK-PEA PATÉ)
(Serves 4)

Preparation Time in a Crock Pot: 8 to 10 hours

1 jar Middle East Style	1 cup tahini
Chick-Pea Mix	¼ cup olive oil
4 cups water	2 tablespoons lemon juice

Remove seasoning and place in ¼ cup water. Set aside.
Place chick-peas and remaining water in an electric crock pot. Set on high and cook, covered, for 8 to 10 hours while at

work or overnight. Stir in seasoning in water. Cook for 15 minutes. Add tahini, olive oil and lemon juice. Puree in a food processor or electric blender. Serve with whole wheat buns or pita.

Preparation Time in a Pot: 4½ hours

1 jar Middle East Style
   Chick-Pea Mix
4½ cups water

1 cup tahini
¼ cup olive oil
2 tablespoons lemon juice

Remove seasoning and set aside.

Place chick-peas and water in a covered pot. Boil for 10 minutes. Reduce heat to medium low. Stir in seasoning. Cook, covered, for 4 hours until soft. Remove from heat and stir in tahini, olive oil and lemon juice. Puree in a food processor or electric blender.

This dish may be used as a dip for whole wheat buns or pita.

Preparation Time in a Pressure Cooker: 2¼ hours

1 jar Middle East Style
   Chick-Pea Mix
3½ cups water

1 cup tahini
¼ cup olive oil
2 tablespoons lemon juice

Place seasoning mixture, chick-peas and water in a pressure cooker. Cover and cook over high heat until pressure reaches 15 pounds. Reduce heat to low and cook for 2 hours. Decrease pressure according to manufacturer's instructions. Remove from heat and stir in tahini, olive oil and lemon juice. Puree in a food processor or electric blender.

CHICK-PEA SALAD (*Serves 4*)

Preparation Time: 10 minutes

3 cups cooked Middle East
  Chick-Pea Mix (p. 95)
1 green pepper, chopped

1 onion, chopped
2 teaspoons cider vinegar
⅓ cup olive oil

In a bowl, combine chick-peas, green pepper and onion. Pour vinegar and olive oil over mixture and toss until thoroughly coated.

CHICK-PEA AND BULGUR SALAD (*Serves 4 to 6*)

Preparation Time: 10 minutes

3 cups cooked Middle East
Chick-Peas (p. 95)
1½ cups cooked bulgur
2 tomatoes, chopped

1 onion, chopped
3 teaspoons lemon juice
⅓ cup olive oil
1 tablespoon tahini

In a bowl, combine chick-peas, bulgur, tomatoes and onion. In a separate small bowl, beat lemon juice, olive oil and tahini until smooth. Pour over salad and toss until well coated.

BASIC EUROPEAN LENTIL MIX
(*Makes five 12-ounce jars; each jar serves 4*)

5 cups lentils
1 cup dried minced onion
5 teaspoons celery seed

½ cup dried parsley
2½ teaspoons basil
2 teaspoons garlic powder

2½ teaspoons salt (optional)

Measure 1 cup beans into 5 wide-mouth jars. In a small bowl, combine remaining ingredients and mix thoroughly. Spoon 6 tablespoons of this seasoning mixture into 5 small plastic bags and place 1 bag in each jar. Seal jars tightly and store in cool dark cupboard. Use within two months.

LENTIL STEW (Serves 4)

Preparation Time in a Crock Pot: 8 to 10 hours

1 jar European Lentil Mix   3 cups water

Remove seasoning and place in ⅓ cup water. Set aside. Place lentils and remaining 2⅔ cups water in an electric crock pot. Set on high and cook, covered, for 8 to 10 hours while at work or overnight. Stir in seasoning in water. Cook for 15 minutes before serving.

Preparation Time in a Pot: 40 minutes

1 jar European Lentil Mix   3¼ cups water

Remove seasoning and set aside. Place lentils and water in a covered pot. Boil for 10 minutes. Reduce heat to medium low.
Stir in seasoning and cook, covered, for 30 minutes until soft.

Preparation Time in a Pressure Cooker: 20 minutes

1 jar European Lentil Mix   3 cups water

Place seasoning mixture, lentils and water in a pressure cooker. Cover and cook over high heat until pressure reaches 15 pounds. Reduce heat to low and cook for 20 minutes. Decrease pressure according to manufacturer's instructions.

LENTIL LOAF (Serves 4)

Preparation and Baking Time: 45 minutes

2 cups leftover European   1 cup whole wheat, oat or rice
Lentil Stew (previous   flour
recipe)

Combine leftover stew with flour to form a stiff mixture.
Turn into an oiled loaf pan. Bake for 45 minutes at 350 degrees. Remove from pan. Serve hot with a sauce or gravy or cold in sandwiches.

LENTIL CRUMB CASSEROLE (*Serves 4*)

Baking Time: 20 minutes

2 cups leftover Lentil Stew (p. 100)

1½ cups whole grain bread crumbs

2 tablespoons butter

Mix leftover stew with ½ cup bread crumbs. Turn into an oiled casserole. Sprinkle with remaining bread crumbs and dot with butter.

Bake at 350 degrees for 20 minutes until topping is lightly browned.

LENTIL CHEESE CASSEROLE (*Serves 4*)

Baking Time: 20 minutes

2 cups leftover Lentil Stew (p. 100)

1½ cups grated Cheddar cheese

Mix leftover stew with ¾ cup of the cheese. Turn into an oiled casserole dish. Sprinkle with remaining cheese and bake at 350 degrees for 20 minutes, or until cheese is melted, before serving.

LENTIL CROQUETTES (*Serves 4 to 6*)

Preparation Time: 15 minutes

2 cups cooked Lentil Stew (p. 100)

1 cup whole wheat flour

1 tablespoon oil

In a bowl, mix stew and flour to form a stiff dough. With moistened hands, shape into patties.

In a frying pan, heat oil over medium-high heat. Fry patties on both sides until golden brown.

Serve with sauce or gravy.

LENTIL SALAD (*Serves 4 to 6*)

Preparation Time: 10 minutes

2 cups cooked Lentil Stew   1 green pepper, chopped
  (p. 100)   1 tomato, chopped
¼ cup chopped parsley   2 celery stalks, diced
2 onions, finely chopped   1 tablespoon cider vinegar
¼ cup olive oil

In a bowl, combine cooked stew, parsley, onions, green pepper, tomato and diced celery.

Sprinkle with cider vinegar and oil. Toss until mixture is well distributed.

LENTIL POT PIE (*Serves 4*)

Preparation and Baking Time: 50 minutes

2½ cups cooked Lentil Stew   ½ cup chopped green
  (p. 100)   peppers
1 cup corn kernels   1 recipe Rolled Biscuits
1 cup chopped celery   (p. 163) (unbaked)

Combine stew, corn, celery and green peppers. Pour mixture into a well-oiled casserole dish.

Top with unbaked Rolled Biscuits and bake at 400 degrees for 30 minutes until golden brown.

LENTIL SHEPHERD'S PIE (*Serves 4 to 6*)

Preparation and Baking Time: 55 minutes

3 cups cooked Lentil Stew   2 cups leftover mashed
  (p. 100)   potatoes
2 cups corn kernels

Combine lentil stew and corn kernels. Pour into a well-oiled casserole or loaf pan. Top with mashed potatoes. Bake for 40 minutes until top of potatoes is lightly browned and crusted.

BASIC KIDNEY BEAN MIX
(Makes five 12-ounce jars; each jar serves 4)

5 cups dried kidney beans	2½ teaspoons rosemary
⅔ cup dried minced onion	1¼ teaspoons black pepper
⅓ cup dried parsley	2½ teaspoons oregano
5 teaspoons dried minced garlic	2½ teaspoons salt (optional)

Measure 1 cup beans into each of 5 wide-mouth jars. In a small bowl, combine remaining ingredients and mix thoroughly. Spoon 4 tablespoons of this seasoning mixture into 5 small plastic bags and place 1 bag in each jar. Seal jars tightly and store in cool dark cupboard. Use within two months.

KIDNEY BEAN STEW *(Serves 4)*

Preparation Time in a Crock Pot: 8 to 10 hours

1 jar Kidney Bean Mix   3¾ cups water

Empty bag of seasoning into ¼ cup water. Stir and set aside. Pour beans and 3½ cups water into an electric crock pot. Set on high and cook, covered, for 8 to 10 hours while at work or overnight. Stir in seasoning in water 15 minutes before serving.

Preparation Time in a Pot: 3½ hours

1 jar Kidney Bean Mix   4 cups water

Remove plastic bag containing seasoning and set aside. In a covered pot, boil water and beans for 10 minutes. Reduce heat to medium low. Cook for 3 hours. Stir in seasoning and cook for 20 minutes more before serving.

Preparation Time in a Pressure Cooker: 1½ hours

1 jar Kidney Bean Mix   3½ cups water

Place seasoning mixture, beans and water in a pressure cooker. Cover and cook on high heat until pressure is increased to 15 pounds. Reduce heat to low and cook for 1¼ hours. Decrease pressure according to manufacturer's instructions. Serve with rice or topped with grated cheese for a balanced protein main dish.

KIDNEY BEAN DINNER SALAD (*Serves 4 to 6*)

Preparation Time: 15 minutes

2 cups cooked Kidney Bean   1 onion, chopped
  Stew (previous recipe)   3 scallions, chopped
1 cup cooked bulgur   ¼ cup chopped parsley
2 tomatoes, chopped   2 tablespoons lemon juice
                    ⅓ cup olive oil

In a bowl, combine cooked kidney stew, bulgur, tomatoes, onion, scallions and parsley. Pour lemon juice and olive oil over mixture and toss well before serving.

BAKED KIDNEY BEAN, TOMATO AND ONION CASSEROLE (*Serves 4 to 6*)

Preparation Time: 5 minutes
Cooking Time: 6 hours (in an oven); 8 to 10 hours (in an electric crock pot)

1 jar Kidney Bean Mix   4 whole tomatoes, peeled
4 cups water   8 small whole onions

Remove seasoning packet. Place seasoning in ⅓ cup water and set aside.

In a casserole or crock pot, combine beans, remaining 3⅔ cups water, tomatoes and onions. Bake in a covered casserole in an oven at 350 degrees for 5 hours, then mix in seasoning and bake for a final hour. Or set crock pot on high and cook for 8 to 10 hours. Stir in seasoning and cook for a final 15 minutes.

KIDNEY BEAN STUFFED PUMPKIN (*Serves 6 to 8*)

Preparation and Baking Time: 1¾ hours

1 recipe Baked Kidney Bean,   1 medium-size pumpkin
Tomato and Onion Casserole   3 tablespoons oil
(previous recipe)

Prepare previous recipe. Preheat oven to 375 degrees.

Cut stem out of pumpkin, reserving it. Clean pulp and seeds from inside. Oil pumpkin shell inside and out.

Replace stem and bake for 45 minutes until shell can be pierced with a fork but is still firm. Spoon casserole recipe into pumpkin shell.

Bake for 30 minutes longer before serving on a large platter.

KIDNEY BEANS IN TOMATO SAUCE (*Serves 4*)

Preparation Time in a Crock Pot: 8 to 10 hours

1 jar Kidney Bean Mix   3¾ cups water
3 tablespoons tomato paste

Remove seasoning and place in ¼ cup water. Set aside.

Place beans and remaining 3½ cups water in an electric crock pot. Set on high and cook, covered, for 8 to 10 hours while at work or overnight.

Stir in seasoning in water and tomato paste. Cook for 15 minutes before serving.

Preparation Time in a Pot: 4 ½ ours

1 jar Kidney Bean Mix   4 cups water
3 tablespoons tomato paste

Remove seasoning and set aside. Place beans and water in a covered pot. Boil for 10 minutes. Reduce heat to medium low and cook for 3½ hours until soft. Stir in seasoning and tomato paste. Cook for 30 minutes before serving.

Preparation Time in a Pressure Cooker: 1½ hours

1 jar Kidney Bean Mix   3 cups water
3 tablespoons tomato paste

Place seasoning mixture, beans and water in a pressure cooker. Cover and cook over high heat until pressure reaches 15 pounds. Reduce heat to low and cook for 1¼ hours. Decrease pressure according to manufacturer's instructions. Stir in tomato paste before serving.

KIDNEY BEANS IN SOUR CREAM SAUCE WITH WHOLE POTATOES (*Serves 4*)

Preparation Time in a Crock Pot: 8 to 10 hours

1 jar Kidney Bean Mix   8 small whole potatoes,
4 cups water   unpeeled
1 cup sour cream

Remove seasoning and place in ½ cup water. Set aside.
Place beans, potatoes and remaining 3½ cups water in an electric crock pot. Set on high and cook, covered, for 8 to 10 hours while at work or overnight. Stir in seasoning in water and sour cream. Cook for 15 minutes before serving.

Preparation Time in a Pot: 3½ hours

1 jar Kidney Bean Mix
4½ cups water

8 small whole potatoes, unpeeled
1 cup sour cream

Remove seasoning and set aside.
Place beans, water and potatoes in covered pot. Boil for 10 minutes. Reduce heat to medium low.
Cook, covered, for 3 hours until beans are soft. Stir in seasoning and sour cream and cook for 20 minutes before serving.

Preparation Time in a Pressure Cooker: 1½ hours

1 jar Kidney Bean Mix
3 cups water

8 small whole potatoes, unpeeled
1 cup sour cream

Place seasoning mixture, beans, water and potatoes in a pressure cooker. Cover and cook over high heat until pressure reaches 15 pounds. Reduce heat to low and cook for 1½ hours. Decrease pressure according to manufacturer's instructions. Stir in sour cream before serving.

KIDNEY BEANS IN CHEESE SAUCE (*Serves 4*)

Preparation Time in a Crock Pot: 8 to 10 hours

1 jar Kidney Bean Mix
4 cups water

½ cup yogurt or sour cream
1 cup grated Cheddar cheese

Remove seasoning and place in ½ cup water. Set aside.
Place beans and remaining 3½ cups water in an electric crock pot. Set on high and cook, covered, for 8 to 10 hours while at work or overnight.
Stir in seasoning in water, yogurt or sour cream and Cheddar cheese. Cook for 15 minutes before serving.

Preparation Time in a Pot: 4 hours

1 jar Kidney Bean Mix	½ cup yogurt or sour cream
4½ cups water	1 cup grated Cheddar cheese

Remove seasoning and set aside.
Place beans and water in a covered pot. Boil for 10 minutes. Reduce heat to medium low. Cook for 3½ hours until beans are soft. Stir in seasoning, sour cream or yogurt and Cheddar cheese. Cook for 15 minutes, stirring occasionally, until sauce forms.

Preparation Time in a Pressure Cooker: 1½ hours

1 jar Kidney Bean Mix	½ cup yogurt or sour cream
3 cups water	1 cup grated Cheddar cheese

Place seasoning mixture, beans and water in a pressure cooker. Cover and cook over high heat until pressure reaches 15 pounds. Reduce heat to low and cook for 1¼ hours. Decrease pressure according to manufacturer's instructions.
Stir in sour cream or yogurt and grated cheese, to form a sauce before serving.

KIDNEY BEAN AND EGG CASSEROLE (*Serves 4 to 6*)

Preparation and Baking Time: 35 minutes

8 hard-boiled eggs	1 cup whole grain bread
1 recipe Kidney Beans in	crumbs
Cheese Sauce (previous	1 tablespoon butter
recipe)	

Slice eggs thin. Prepare previous recipe. Preheat oven to 400 degrees.
In an oiled casserole dish, spread ⅓ of bean mixture, cover with a layer of 3 sliced eggs. Repeat layers and top with a layer of beans. Sprinkle bread crumbs over top and dot with butter. Reserve two sliced eggs for garnish.

Bake for 25 minutes until top is golden brown. Place sliced eggs around edge just before serving.

BASIC MEXICAN PINTO BEAN MIX
(Makes five 12-ounce jars; each jar serves 4)

5 cups pinto beans	5 teaspoons ground cumin
5 tablespoons dried minced onion	5 teaspoons chili powder
	2½ teaspoons black pepper
5 tablespoons dried minced garlic	2½ teaspoons salt (optional)

Measure 1 cup beans into each of 5 wide-mouth jars.

In a small bowl, mix remaining ingredients until thoroughly combined. Spoon 3 tablespoons (plus ½ teaspoon if including salt) of this seasoning mixture into 5 small plastic bags and place 1 bag in each jar. Seal jars tightly and store in cool dark cupboard. Use within two months.

MEXICAN PINTO BEANS (Serves 4)

Preparation Time in a Crock Pot: 8 to 10 hours

1 jar Mexican Pinto Bean Mix	3¾ cups water

Remove seasoning and place in ¼ cup water. Set aside.

Place beans and remaining 3½ cups water in an electric crock pot. Set on high and cook, covered, for 8 to 10 hours while at work or overnight. Stir in seasoning in water. Cook for 15 minutes before serving.

Preparation Time in a Pot: 3½ hours

1 jar Mexican Pinto Bean Mix   4 cups water

Remove seasoning and set aside. Place beans and water in a covered pot. Boil for 10 minutes. Reduce heat to medium low. Cook for 3 hours until beans are soft. Stir in seasoning and cook for 20 minutes before serving.

Preparation Time in a Pressure Cooker: 1½ hours

1 jar Pinto Bean Mix   2½ cups water

Place seasoning mixture, beans and water in a pressure cooker. Cover and cook over high heat until pressure reaches 15 pounds. Reduce heat to low and cook for 1¼ hours. Decrease pressure according to manufacturer's instructions.

TACOS (Serves 4)

Preparation Time: 15 minutes

1 tablespoon oil   8 taco shells
2 cups cooked Mexican Pinto   1 cup shredded lettuce
  Beans (previous recipe)   1 cup grated Cheddar cheese
          ½ cup chopped tomatoes

In a frying pan, heat oil over medium heat. Stir in cooked pinto beans and cook until any excess water evaporates.

Fill each taco shell with ¼ cup of heated mixture. Top with layers of lettuce, Cheddar cheese and chopped tomatoes.

BURRITOS (*Serves 4*)

Preparation Time: 15 minutes

2 cups cooked Mexican Pinto   4 flour tortillas
Beans (p. 109)   1 cup hot sauce

Reheat leftover pinto beans. Heat tortillas in a 350 degree oven for 5 minutes. To assemble, place ½ cup of reheated beans in a line across the warm tortilla. Roll the tortilla around the beans. This dish may be served with hot sauce.

ENCHILADA CASSEROLE (*Serves 4*)

Preparation Time: 30 minutes

2 cups cooked Mexican Pinto   4 corn tortillas
Beans (p. 109)   1 cup grated Cheddar cheese

In a casserole dish spread a thin layer of pinto beans. Top with a tortilla. Make a layer of pinto beans, then of grated cheese. Add another tortilla and repeat layers until all ingredients are used, ending with a layer of cheese.

Bake uncovered at 350 degrees for 20 minutes until all cheese is melted.

PINTO BEAN AND CHEESE CASSEROLE (*Serves 4*)

Preparation Time: 30 minutes

2 cups cooked Mexican   1½ cups grated Cheddar
Pinto Beans (p. 109)   cheese

Arrange beans and cheese in layers in an oiled casserole, ending with a layer of cheese.

Bake at 350 degrees for 20 minutes until thoroughly heated before serving.

MEXICAN BEAN DIP (*Makes 2 cups*)

Preparation Time: 3 minutes

2 cups cooked Mexican Pinto Beans (p. 109)

Puree cooked beans in a blender or food processor. This dip may be served with tortilla chips, used as an appetizer or as the main course of a summer lunch.

REFRIED BEANS (*Serves 4*)

2 tablespoons olive oil   1 jar cooked Mexican Pinto
                                 Beans (p. 109)

Heat oil over medium burner in a heavy frying pan. Add cooked pinto beans. Stir until excess liquid has cooked off and beans have become creamy with a lighter color. This dish may be served alone or with rice.

MEXICAN STEW (*Serves 4*)

Preparation Time in a Crock Pot: 4 to 10 hours

1 jar Mexican Pinto Bean Mix   ½ cup corn kernels
6 cups water   ½ cup zucchini, cut in 2-inch
2 carrots, cut in 2-inch chunks   chunks

Remove seasoning and place in ½ cup water. Set aside.

Place beans, vegetables and remaining 5½ cups water in an electric crock pot. Set on high and cook, covered, for 8 to 10 hours while at work or overnight. Stir in seasoning in water. Cook for 15 minutes before serving.

Preparation Time in a Pot: 4 hours

1 jar Mexican Pinto Bean
  Mix
6½ cups water
2 carrots, cut in 2-inch
  chunks

½ cup zucchini, cut in 2-inch
  chunks
½ cup corn kernels

Remove seasoning and set aside. Place beans and water in a covered pot. Boil for 10 minutes. Reduce heat to medium low. Stir in seasoning and vegetables. Cook, covered, for 3¾ hours until soft.

Preparation Time in a Pressure Cooker: 1½ hours

1 jar Mexican Pinto Bean
  Mix
4½ cups water

½ cup corn kernels
2 carrots, cut in 2-inch
  chunks

½ cup zucchini, cut in 2-inch chunks

Place seasoning mixture, beans, water and vegetables in a pressure cooker. Cover and cook over high heat until pressure reaches 15 pounds. Reduce heat to low and cook for 1¼ hours. Decrease pressure according to manufacturer's instructions.

CHAPTER SIX

Rice and Other Grain Mixes

Vitamin-B packed whole grains are the protein complements of legumes, and when eaten in conjunction with them, the combination provides protein as complete as that found in meat, fish, eggs and dairy products.

The grain mixes in this chapter include only whole grains since these are of undeniably greater nutritional value than refined grains. For the busy cook, we introduce basmati rice as a quick cooking alternative to brown rice. Basmati rice is a naturally white grain. It cooks in 20 minutes and has the appearance of white refined rice while retaining all the nutrition of a whole grain. A delicate strain of rice, it is difficult to grow and viewed as a great delicacy in India, its country of origin. Recently, basmati rice has been imported and is becoming readily available in both natural food stores and Indian food shops. Although slightly more expensive than brown rice, its quick cooking advantage makes it desirable for many cooks.

Other grain mixes include millet, bulgur and kasha (buckwheat groats). These three grains are readily available at natural food stores, health food stores and sometimes in the health food or specialty sections of large supermarkets. All three can be prepared in under 25 minutes, making them perfect candidates for versatile homemade mixes.

All grain mixes are stored in 12-ounce or pint-size jars. Spices and flavorings are measured directly in the jars, which are designed to serve four people. This method of storage assures that whatever variation of a mix is being served each mix will be properly spiced or seasoned.

BASIC INDIAN RICE PILAF MIX
(Makes six 12-ounce jars; each jar serves 4)

8 cups brown rice or basmati rice	1 tablespoon paprika
6 tablespoons dried minced onion	1 tablespoon ground cardamom
1 tablespoon dried minced garlic	2 tablespoons garam masala
1½ teaspoons ground cloves	2 tablespoons ground cumin
1 tablespoon ground cinnamon	2 tablespoons ground coriander
	1½ teaspoons ground ginger

1 tablespoon salt (optional)

Measure 1⅓ cups rice into each of six 12-ounce jars. Mix the remaining ingredients in a separate bowl until thoroughly combined. Spoon 3 tablespoons of this mixture into each jar. Seal tightly and store in a cool dark cupboard. Use within three months.

INDIAN RICE PILAF (Serves 4)

Preparation Time: 45 minutes for brown rice;
20 minutes for basmati rice

1 jar Indian Rice Pilaf Mix   2¾ cups water

In a covered pot, combine mix and water. Bring to a boil. Reduce heat to low and cook, covered, for 40 to 45 minutes, if using brown rice, or 20 minutes if using basmati rice.

CREAM CURRIED RICE (Serves 4)

Preparation Time: 50 minutes for brown rice;
25 minutes for basmati rice

1 jar Indian Rice Pilaf Mix   ½ cup sour cream mixed with
2¾ cups water   2 tablespoons water

In a covered pot, combine mix and water. Bring to a boil. Reduce heat to low and cook, covered, for 45 minutes, if using brown rice, or 20 minutes if using basmati rice.

Stir in sour cream and water mixture just before serving.

TOMATO RICE CURRY (Serves 4)

Preparation Time: 50 minutes for brown rice;
25 minutes for basmati rice

1 jar Indian Rice Pilaf Mix   2⅔ cups water
                    ½ cup tomato juice

In a covered pot, combine rice mix and water. Bring to a boil. Reduce heat to low and cook, covered, for 40 minutes, if using brown rice, or 15 minutes if using basmati rice.

Stir in tomato juice and cook, covered, for 10 minutes before serving.

FRUIT CURRIED RICE (Serves 4)

Preparation Time: 50 minutes for brown rice;
25 minutes for basmati rice

1 jar Indian Rice Pilaf Mix   1 orange, sectioned, with
¼ cup raisins   membranes removed
2¾ cups water   3 tablespoons orange juice

In a covered pot, combine rice mix, raisins and water. Bring to a boil. Reduce heat to low and cook, covered, for

45 minutes, if using brown rice, or 20 minutes if using basmati rice.

Stir in orange sections and orange juice, cover, and cook for 3 minutes before serving.

PEAS PILAF (*Serves 4*)

Preparation Time: 55 minutes for brown rice;
30 minutes for basmati rice

1 jar Indian Rice Pilaf Mix	2 tablespoons butter
2¾ cups water	½ cup peas (fresh or frozen)

In a covered pot, combine rice mix and water. Bring to a boil and reduce heat to low. Cook, covered, for 45 minutes, if using brown rice, or 20 minutes if using basmati rice.

In a heavy frying pan, melt butter over medium-high heat. Stir-fry peas until bright green in color but still crisp. Stir in rice, coating it thoroughly with butter.

MUSHROOM PILAF (*Serves 4*)

Preparation Time: 55 minutes for brown rice;
30 minutes for basmati rice

1 jar Indian Rice Pilaf Mix	2 tablespoons butter
2¾ cups water	1 cup sliced fresh mushrooms

In a covered pot, combine mix and water. Bring to a boil. Reduce heat to low and cook, covered, for 45 minutes, if using brown rice, or 20 minutes if using basmati rice.

In a heavy frying pan, melt butter over medium-high heat. Stir in mushrooms. Sauté until decreased in size and darkened in color. Stir in cooked rice mix just before serving.

LENTIL RICE PILAF (*Serves 4 to 6*)

Preparation Time: 50 minutes

⅓ cup lentils   3¾ cups water
                    1 jar Indian Rice Pilaf Mix

In a covered pot, combine lentils, water and rice mix. Bring to a boil. Reduce heat to low and cook for 45 minutes until rice is tender and lentils are soft.

YELLOW PEA RICE PILAF (*Serves 4 to 6*)

Preparation Time: 50 minutes

¼ cup dried yellow split peas   3¾ cups water
                    1 jar Indian Rice Pilaf Mix

In a covered pot, combine peas, water and rice mix. Bring to a boil. Reduce heat to low and cook for 45 minutes until rice is tender and peas are soft.

CURRIED RICE WITH ALMONDS (*Serves 4*)

Preparation Time: 50 minutes for brown rice;
25 minutes for basmati rice

½ cup whole almonds   2¾ cups water
                    1 jar Indian Rice Pilaf Mix

In a covered pot, combine almonds, water and rice. Bring to a boil. Reduce heat and cook, covered, for 45 minutes, if using brown rice, or 20 minutes if using basmati rice.

EGGPLANT CURRIED RICE (Serves 4)

Preparation Time: 50 minutes for brown rice;
25 minutes for basmati rice

½ cup peeled and chopped   3 cups water
   eggplant   1 jar Indian Rice Pilaf Mix

In a covered pot, combine eggplant, water and rice mix. Bring to a boil. Reduce heat to low and cook, covered, for 45 minutes, if using brown rice, or 20 minutes if using basmati rice.

BASIC MIDDLE EASTERN RICE PILAF MIX
(Makes six 12-ounce jars; each jar serves 4)

8 cups brown rice or bismati   6 tablespoons toasted sesame
   rice   seeds
2 tablespoons dried mint   2 tablespoons ground cumin
1 tablespoon garlic powder   1 teaspoon ground coriander
1 teaspoon cayenne   1 teaspoon salt (optional)

Measure 1⅓ cups rice into six 12-ounce jars. In a bowl, combine remaining ingredients and mix thoroughly. Measure 2 tablespoons of mixture into each jar. Seal tightly and store in cool dark cupboard. Use within two months.

MIDDLE EASTERN FLAVORED RICE (Serves 4)

Preparation Time: 50 minutes for brown rice;
25 minutes for basmati rice

1 jar Middle Eastern Rice   2¾ cups water
   Pilaf Mix

In a covered pot, combine rice mix and water. Bring to a boil. Reduce heat to low and cook, covered, for 45 minutes, if using brown rice, or 20 minutes if using basmati rice.

MIDDLE EASTERN RICE IN TAHINI SAUCE
(*Serves 4*)

Preparation Time: 55 minutes for brown rice;
30 minutes for basmati rice

1 jar Middle Eastern Rice
Pilaf Mix
2¾ cups water

2 tablespoons tahini mixed
with 2 tablespoons lemon
juice until smooth

In a covered pot, combine rice mix and water. Bring to a boil. Reduce heat to low and cook, covered, for 45 minutes, if using brown rice, or 20 minutes if using basmati rice.

Stir in tahini-lemon juice paste just before serving.

SESAME RICE YOGURT (*Serves 4*)

Preparation Time: 50 minutes for brown rice;
25 minutes for basmati rice

1 jar Middle Eastern Rice
Pilaf Mix
2⅔ cups water

1 cup yogurt mixed with 2
tablespoons water

In a pot, combine rice mix and water. Bring to a boil. Reduce heat to low. Cook, covered, for 45 minutes, if using brown rice, or 20 minutes if using basmati rice.

Stir in yogurt-and-water mixture just before serving.

MIDDLE EASTERN RICE IN TOMATO SAUCE
(*Serves 4*)

Preparation Time: 55 minutes for brown rice;
30 minutes for basmati rice

1 jar Middle Eastern Rice
Pilaf Mix

2⅓ cups water
⅔ cup tomato juice

In a covered pot, combine rice mix and water. Bring to a boil. Reduce heat to low and cook, covered, for 40 minutes, if using brown rice, or 15 minutes if using basmati rice.

Add tomato juice and cook for 10 minutes longer.

MIDDLE EASTERN RICE WITH EGGPLANT
(*Serves 4*)

Preparation Time: 50 minutes for brown rice;
25 minutes for basmati rice

1 jar Middle Eastern Rice Pilaf Mix

2¾ cups water
1 eggplant, peeled and diced

In a covered pot, combine mix, water and eggplant. Bring to a boil. Reduce heat to low and cook, covered, for 45 minutes, if using brown rice, or 20 minutes if using basmati rice.

BASIC SPANISH RICE MIX
(*Makes six 12-ounce jars; each jar serves 4*)

8 cups brown rice or basmati rice
7 tablespoons dried minced onion
2 tablespoons dried minced garlic

4 teaspoons crushed red peppers
4 teaspoons ground cumin
1 teaspoon salt (optional)

Measure 1⅓ cups rice into six 12-ounce jars. In a separate bowl, combine the remaining ingredients and mix thoroughly. Spoon 2 tablespoons of mixture into each jar. Seal tightly and store in cool dark cupboard. Use within three months.

SPANISH RICE (Serves 4)

Preparation Time: 50 minutes for brown rice;
25 minutes for basmati rice

1 jar Spanish Rice Mix   2½ cups water
½ cup tomato juice

In a covered pot, combine rice mix and water. Bring to a boil. Reduce heat to low and cook, covered, for 35 minutes, if using brown rice, or 10 minutes if using basmati rice.

Stir in tomato juice and cook for 10 minutes longer.

CREAMY SPANISH RICE (Serves 4)

Preparation Time: 50 minutes for brown rice;
25 minutes for basmati rice

1 jar Spanish Rice Mix   ½ cup tomato juice
2⅔ cups water   ⅔ cup sour cream

In a covered pot, combine rice mix and water. Bring to a boil. Reduce heat to low and cook, covered, for 45 minutes, if using brown rice, or 20 minutes if using basmati rice.

Stir in tomato juice and sour cream just before serving.

SPICY RICE (Serves 4)

Preparation Time: 50 minutes for brown rice;
25 minutes for basmati rice

1 jar Spanish Rice Mix   2¾ cups water

In a covered pot, combine rice mix and water. Bring to a boil. Reduce heat to low and cook for 45 minutes, if using brown rice, or 20 minutes if using basmati rice.

CHEESY SPANISH RICE (Serves 4)

Preparation Time: 55 minutes for brown rice;
30 minutes for basmati rice

1 jar Spanish Rice Mix
2½ cups water

½ cup tomato juice
½ cup grated Cheddar cheese

In a covered pot, combine rice mix and water. Bring to a boil. Reduce heat to low and cook, covered, for 35 minutes, if using brown rice, or 10 minutes if using basmati rice.

Stir in tomato juice and cook for 10 minutes longer. Just before serving stir in cheese until it melts.

BASIC MIDDLE EASTERN BULGUR MIX
(Makes 6 pint jars; each jar serves 4)

8 cups bulgur
1½ cups toasted sesame seeds
3 tablespoons dried minced garlic

7 teaspoons ground cumin
1 teaspoon cayenne
1 teaspoon salt (optional)

Measure 1⅓ cups bulgur into 6 pint jars. In a bowl, combine the remaining ingredients and mix thoroughly. Spoon 5 tablespoons of this mixture into each jar. Seal tightly and store in cool dark cupboard. Use within three months.

MIDDLE EASTERN BULGUR (Serves 4)

Preparation Time: 25 minutes

2¾ cups water

1 jar Middle Eastern Bulgur Mix

In a covered pot, bring water to a boil. Add bulgur mix, cover again, and reduce heat to low. Cook for 20 to 25 minutes until bulgur is fluffy.

BULGUR WITH TAHINI SAUCE (Serves 4)

Preparation Time: 35 minutes

2¾ cups water
1 jar Middle Eastern Bulgur
Mix

3 tablespoons tahini mixed
with 2 tablespoons lemon
juice until smooth

In a pot, bring water to a boil. Add bulgur mix, cover, and reduce heat to low. Cook for 20 to 25 minutes until bulgur is fluffy.

Stir in tahini-lemon juice paste just before serving.

BULGUR WITH YOGURT SAUCE (Serves 4)

Preparation Time: 35 minutes

2¾ cups water

1 jar Middle Eastern Bulgur
Mix

1 cup yogurt

In a pot, bring water to a boil. Add mix, cover, and reduce heat to low. Simmer for 20 to 25 minutes until bulgur is fluffy.

Stir in yogurt and cook for 5 minutes until thoroughly heated before serving.

BULGUR IN TOMATO SAUCE (Serves 4)

Preparation Time: 30 minutes

2½ cups water
1 jar Middle Eastern Bulgur
Mix

½ cup tomato juice
2 tomatoes, finely chopped

In a pot, bring water to a boil. Add bulgur mix, cover, and reduce heat to low. Cook for 15 minutes.

Stir in tomato juice and tomatoes and cook for 10 minutes longer until bulgur is tender.

QUICK BULGUR CASSEROLE (*Serves 4*)

Preparation Time: 15 minutes

1 recipe Bulgur in Tomato   ⅔ cup grated Cheddar cheese
Sauce (previous recipe)

Turn bulgur with tomato sauce into an oiled casserole dish. Sprinkle with Cheddar cheese and bake for 10 minutes at 400 degrees until cheese has melted.

TABULE (*Serves 4*)

Preparation Time: 35 minutes

2¾ cups water   ½ cup chopped green
  1 jar Middle Eastern Bulgur   peppers
     Mix   ⅔ cup chopped tomatoes
⅓ cup chopped scallions   2 teaspoons lemon juice
        ¼ cup olive oil

In a pot, boil water. Add bulgur mix, cover, and reduce heat to low. Cook for 20 to 25 minutes until bulgur is fluffy.

Remove from heat and pour into a large bowl. Combine with scallions, green peppers and tomatoes. Pour lemon juice and olive oil over vegetables. Toss well before serving warm or cold.

BASIC SPICED KASHA MIX
(*Makes 6 pint jars; each jar serves 4*)

   8 cups roasted kasha   2 tablespoons dried minced
1½ cups dried minced onion   garlic
  1 tablespoon paprika   1½ teaspoons black pepper
      1½ teaspoons salt (optional)

Measure 1⅓ cups kasha into each of 6 pint jars. In a separate bowl, combine remaining ingredients and mix thoroughly. Spoon ¼ cup of mixture into each jar. Cover tightly and store in cool dark cupboard. Use within three months.

SPICED KASHA (Serves 4)

Preparation Time: 25 minutes

2¾ cups water   1 jar Spiced Kasha Mix

In a pot, bring water to a boil. Add kasha mix, cover, and reduce heat to low. Cook for 20 minutes until kasha is soft.

KASHA LOAF (Serves 4 to 6)

Preparation and Baking Time: 55 minutes

3 cups water   2 eggs, beaten
1 jar Spiced Kasha Mix   ½ cup whole wheat flour

In a pot, bring water to a boil. Add kasha mix, cover, and reduce heat to low. Cook for 20 minutes until kasha is tender. Preheat oven to 400 degrees.

Mix kasha with eggs and flour. Pour into a well-oiled loaf pan and bake for 30 minutes until firm.

This loaf may be served sliced, with gravy or sauce.

BUCKWHEAT PATTIES (Serves 4)

Preparation Time: 30 minutes

2¾ cups water   2 eggs, beaten
1 jar Spiced Kasha Mix   ¼ cup whole wheat flour
1 tablespoon butter

In a pot, bring water to a boil. Add kasha mix, cover, and reduce heat to low. Cook for 20 minutes until kasha is soft.

Remove from heat and beat in eggs and flour. With moistened hands form mixture into patties.

Melt butter in a heavy frying pan and fry patties on both sides until lightly browned.

KASHA AND CARROTS (*Serves 4*)

Preparation Time: 25 minutes

2¾ cups water   ½ cup grated carrots
                    1 jar Spiced Kasha Mix

In a pot, bring water to a boil. Add carrots and kasha. Cover, reduce heat to low, and cook for 20 minutes until kasha is fluffy.

QUICK KASHA CASSEROLE (*Serves 4*)

Preparation Time: 30 minutes

2¾ cups water   1 jar Spiced Kasha Mix
½ cup grated carrots   ⅔ cup grated Cheddar cheese

In a pot, bring water to a boil. Add carrots and kasha mix. Cover, reduce heat to low and cook for 20 minutes until kasha is fluffy.

Turn into a casserole dish, sprinkle with cheese and place under a broiler until cheese has melted.

KASHA IN YOGURT (*Serves 4*)

Preparation Time: 25 minutes

2¾ cups water   1 jar Spiced Kasha Mix
                   1 cup yogurt

In a pot, bring water to a boil. Add kasha mix, cover, and reduce heat to low. Cook for 20 minutes until kasha is fluffy. Stir in yogurt just before serving.

KASHA IN TOMATO SAUCE (Serves 4)

Preparation Time: 30 minutes

2½ cups water
 1 jar Spiced Kasha Mix

⅔ cup tomato juice
 2 tomatoes, finely chopped

In a pot, bring water to a boil. Add kasha mix, cover, and reduce heat to low. Cook for 15 minutes. Add tomato juice and tomatoes and cook for 10 minutes longer.

BASIC HERB 'N ONION MILLET MIX
(*Makes six 12-ounce jars; each jar serves 4*)

6 cups millet
1 cup dried minced onion
½ cup nutritional yeast

½ cup dill seed
1 cup parsley

Measure 1 cup millet into each of six 12-ounce jars. In a bowl, mix onion, dill, parsley and nutritional yeast until evenly distributed. Measure ½ cup of mixture into each jar. Seal tightly and store in cool dark cupboard. Use within two months.

HERB ONION MILLET (Serves 4)

Preparation Time: 30 minutes

3¼ cups water

1 jar Herb 'n Onion Millet Mix

In a pot, bring water to a boil. Reduce heat and stir in millet mix. Cover and cook for 25 minutes until all liquid is absorbed and millet is fluffy.

MILLET IN TAHINI SAUCE (*Serves 4*)

Preparation Time: 30 minutes

3¼ cups water
1 jar Herb 'n Onion Millet
Mix

¼ cup tahini mixed with 3 tablespoons water until smooth
2 teaspoons lemon juice

In a pot, bring water to a boil. Reduce heat to low and stir in millet mix. Cover and cook for 25 minutes until water is absorbed and millet is fluffy.

Stir in tahini-and-water paste and lemon juice just before serving.

MILLET PATTIES (*Serves 4*)

Preparation Time: 10 minutes

2 cups cooked Millet in Tahini
Sauce (previous recipe)

2 tablespoons soy flour
1 tablespoon nutritional yeast
1 tablespoon butter

In a bowl, mix cooked millet with soy flour and nutritional yeast to form a stiff dough. With moistened hands, form into patties.

In a heavy frying pan, melt butter over medium heat. Fry patties on both sides until golden brown.

TOMATO MILLET (Serves 4)

Preparation Time: 30 minutes

2½ cups water
  1 jar Herb 'n Onion Millet
    Mix

1 cup tomato juice
2 tomatoes, finely chopped

In a pot, bring water to a boil. Reduce heat and add millet mix. Cover and cook for 15 minutes.

Stir in tomato juice and chopped tomatoes. Cover and cook for 10 minutes longer until liquid is absorbed.

TOMATO MILLET CASSEROLE (Serves 4)

Preparation and Baking Time: 45 minutes

3 cups water
1 jar Herb 'n Onion Millet
    Mix
2 tomatoes, finely chopped

½ cup tomato juice
1 cup grated Cheddar cheese
⅔ cup whole grain bread
    crumbs

2 tablespoons melted butter

In a pot, bring water to a boil. Reduce heat to low and stir in millet mix. Cook, covered, for 20 minutes.

Add tomatoes and tomato juice and turn into an oiled casserole dish. Top with cheese and bake at 400 degrees for 15 minutes.

Combine bread crumbs and melted butter and sprinkle over casserole. Place under broiler to brown just before serving.

CHAPTER SEVEN

Yeast and Quick Bread Mixes

This chapter presents the possibility of many kinds of breads from a few mixes. With Basic All-Purpose Whole Wheat Bread Mix, you can make Whole Wheat Bread, French Bread, Pretzels, Bagels, Pecan Rolls and much, much more.

Our yeast mixes employ an unusual but very effective and time-saving method of leavening breads. Instant granular yeast is added directly to flours and other dry ingredients to form bread mixes. The yeast is then activated by adding hot liquid (about 120–130 degrees Fahrenheit) to the mix. Although this temperature would kill yeast if added directly to the liquid, the cooling effect of the flour prevents the yeast from becoming inactive. This simple method enables you to by-pass completely the usual initial step in bread-baking of dissolving yeast in lukewarm liquid and waiting 10 minutes for it to dissolve and bubble.

The dough created by using hot liquid is warm and soft. It is therefore more easily and quickly kneaded than conventional whole grain bread doughs.

Since flour varies tremendously in its ability to absorb liquids, the dough created by this method may, at times, be sticky. If your flour has created a sticky dough, knead whole wheat flour into the dough until you achieve the required texture. Do not knead in more mix, since the yeast in the mix will not activate if it is added after the dough is cool.

The ingredients and methods for making and using quick bread mixes are straightforward and employ no special shopping trips or unusual procedures. However, we recommend finding non-alum baking powders at your health food store or supermarket. Health food and natural food stores always carry this type of baking powder. Often, grocery stores or supermarkets will carry Rumford's baking powder, which is the only non-alum baking powder generally available on the commercial market. Other commercial baking powders contain aluminum sulfate, which is detrimental to health.

BASIC ALL-PURPOSE WHOLE WHEAT BREAD MIX
(*Makes 20 cups mix*)

18 cups whole wheat flour	7 tablespoons instant baking
1 cup non-instant powdered	yeast
milk	4 teaspoons salt or salt
½ cup gluten flour	substitute

In a large bowl, combine all ingredients and mix thoroughly. Place in an airtight canister. Store in cool dry cupboard and use within one month or keep in a refrigerator for two months for maximum nutritional value and to retain yeast's freshness.

WHOLE WHEAT BREAD (*Makes 2 loaves*)

Preparation and Rising Time: 3 hours
Baking Time: 50 minutes

3 tablespoons oil	2 cups hot tap water
2 tablespoons blackstrap	5 cups All-Purpose Whole
molasses	Wheat Bread Mix

In a large bowl, combine oil, blackstrap molasses, and hot water. Quickly stir in mix to form a soft dough.

Turn onto a well-floured board and knead for 10 minutes until dough is soft and elastic. Or knead in three small batches in a food processor, adding more flour if necessary. If dough becomes sticky, knead in additional flour.

Place dough in an oiled bowl, cover with a damp towel and allow to rise in a warm place for 1½ hours until doubled in bulk.

Punch down and form into two loaves. Place in well-oiled loaf pans. Oil the tops of the loaves and allow to rise in a warm place for 1 hour until doubled in bulk once again.

Preheat oven to 325 degrees.

Bake loaves for 50 minutes until water sizzles when sprinkled on the bottom of the pans and bread slips easily out of the pans.

WHOLE WHEAT MILK BREAD (Makes 2 loaves)

Preparation and Rising Time: 3 hours
Baking Time: 1 hour

2¼ cups scalded milk
3 tablespoons liquid barley malt

3 tablespoons oil
5 cups All-Purpose Whole Wheat Bread Mix

In a large bowl, combine hot milk, malt and oil. Quickly stir in mix to form a soft dough.

Turn onto a well-floured board and knead until soft and elastic. Or knead in three small batches in an electric food processor. If dough becomes sticky, knead in additional flour, as needed.

Place ball of dough in an oiled bowl, oil the top of the dough, cover with a warm damp towel and allow to rise in a warm place for 1½ hours or until doubled in bulk.

Punch down dough, form into two loaves and place in loaf pans. Oil the tops of the loaves and allow to rise a second time, until doubled in bulk, for 1 hour.

Preheat oven to 385 degrees.

Bake at 385 for 15 minutes, then reduce heat to 350 and bake for 45 minutes until water sizzles when sprinkled onto the bottom of the pans and bread will slip easily out of the pans.

WHOLE WHEAT CHALLAH (*Makes 1 loaf*)

Preparation and Rising Time: 3 hours
Baking Time: 45 minutes

3 eggs	2 tablespoons maple syrup
¼ cup corn oil	3 to 3½ cups All-Purpose
½ cup hot tap water	Whole Wheat Bread Mix

Separate 1 egg and reserve yolk. Place white, with remaining two eggs, oil, hot water and maple syrup in a mixing bowl. Beat together.

Quickly beat in mix to form a soft dough.

Turn onto a well-floured board and knead for 10 minutes until dough is smooth and elastic. Or knead in three small batches in a food processor. If dough is sticky add more flour as needed. This dough should remain soft and pliable.

Place ball of kneaded dough in an oiled bowl. Coat top of dough with oil, cover with a warm, damp towel and allow to rise in a warm place for 45 minutes or until doubled in bulk.

Punch down and allow to rise once again for 45 minutes.

Punch down and divide into three equal parts. Form each piece into a ball, then roll into strands of equal length. Press strands together at one end, braid them and press together at the other end. Tuck ends under. Place on an oiled cookie sheet.

Beat egg yolk with 1 teaspoon water. Brush on top of braided loaf.

Cover and allow to rise in a warm place for 50 minutes until fully risen.

Preheat oven to 375 degrees and bake for 45 minutes or until golden brown.

WHOLE WHEAT QUICK BREAD (*Makes 2 loaves*)

Preparation and Rising Time: 30 minutes
Baking Time: 40 minutes

2½ cups hot tap water
3 tablespoons liquid barley malt

5 cups All-Purpose Whole Wheat Bread Mix

In a large bowl, combine hot water and malt.

Quickly stir in mix. This dough should be slippery; a substantial portion should stick to a wooden spoon when lifted from the dough; it should not flatten out immediately after mixing and no liquid should be visible around the edge of the bowl. If necessary add more flour or water until this texture is achieved.

Place dough in two well-oiled loaf pans, cover and allow to rise 20 minutes in a warm place.

Preheat oven to 400 degrees.

Bake at 400 for 15 minutes. Reduce heat to 350 degrees and bake for 20 to 25 minutes longer until water sizzles when sprinkled on the bottom of the pans and bread slips easily out of the pans.

WHOLE WHEAT RAISIN CINNAMON BREAD
(Makes 2 loaves)

Preparation and Rising Time: 2 hours
Baking Time: 1 hour

1 egg
2 tablespoons oil
2 cups hot tap water
2 tablespoons blackstrap
  molasses

1 teaspoon ground cinnamon
5 cups All-Purpose Whole
  Wheat Bread Mix
1 cup raisins

In a bowl combine egg, oil, hot water and molasses.

In a separate bowl, combine cinnamon, mix and raisins.

Quickly beat dry ingredients into the liquid with a wooden spoon to form a soft dough.

Turn onto a well-floured board and knead until smooth and elastic. Or knead in three small batches in an electric food processor. If dough is sticky, add more flour as needed.

Shape dough into a ball and place in an oiled bowl. Oil top of dough and cover with a damp, warm towel. Place in a warm spot and allow to rise for 45 minutes until doubled in bulk. Punch down.

Shape into two loaves and place in oiled bread pans. Oil the top of each loaf and allow to rise for 1 hour until again doubled in bulk.

Preheat oven to 400 degrees.

Bake at 400 for 15 minutes. Reduce heat to 350 degrees and bake for 20 to 25 minutes longer until water sizzles when sprinkled on the bottom of the pan and bread slips easily from it.

WHOLE WHEAT ONION BREAD (Makes 2 loaves)

Preparation and Rising Time: 2 hours
Baking Time: 50 minutes

2 cups water
2 tablespoons dried minced onion
1 tablespoon liquid barley malt

3 tablespoons oil
½ cup nutritional yeast
5 cups All-Purpose Whole Wheat Bread Mix

In a saucepan, combine water and dried onion. Cook on medium heat for 10 minutes until onions are tender.

Pour hot water and onion into a large bowl and combine with malt and oil.

In a separate bowl, mix yeast and bread mix.

Beat dry mixture into liquid ingredients until a soft dough is formed. Turn dough onto a well-floured bowl and knead for 10 minutes until smooth and elastic. Or knead in three small batches in an electric food processor. If dough is sticky, add flour as necessary.

Shape dough into a ball and place in an oiled bowl. Oil the top of dough, cover with a warm, damp towel and allow to rise for 45 minutes or until doubled in bulk. Punch down.

Shape into two loaves and place in oiled bread pans. Oil the top of each loaf and allow to rise for 50 minutes until doubled once again.

Preheat oven to 375 degrees.

Bake for 50 minutes until water sizzles when sprinkled on the bottom of the pans and until bread slips easily out of pans.

WHOLE WHEAT FRENCH BREAD (Makes 2 loaves)

Preparation and Rising Time: 2 hours
Baking Time: 40 minutes

1¼ cups boiling water
1 cup yogurt, buttermilk or
whey

5 cups All-Purpose Whole
Wheat Bread Mix

In a bowl, combine water and yogurt, buttermilk or whey to form a hot liquid.

Stir in bread mix to form a dough. Turn onto a floured board and knead for 10 minutes until smooth and elastic. Or knead in three small batches in an electric food processor. This dough should be stiff enough to hold its own shape without the support of a bread pan. If necessary, knead in additional whole wheat flour to achieve this texture.

Form a ball and place dough in an oiled bowl. Oil the top of dough and cover with a warm, damp towel. Allow to rise in a warm place for 45 minutes until doubled in bulk. Punch down.

Divide dough in half. On a floured board roll each half into a rectangle ½-inch thick. Fold the longer sides of each rectangle into the middle. The sides should meet but not overlap. Next, fold the sides over each other. The middle then becomes one edge of the loaf. Pinch the side where the fold is visible and tuck the seam under slightly so that it will not show. Pinch the seams of both ends together also, tucking them under carefully.

Place oblong loaves on an oiled and dusted cookie sheet. Cover with a towel and allow to rise for 1 hour until doubled in bulk.

Preheat oven to 400 degrees.

Using a serrated knife, gently cut diagonal slashes across each loaf, ½-inch deep and 2 inches apart.

Immediately before baking, brush or spray each loaf with water. Bake for 20 minutes and brush or spray with water once again. Bake for a final 25 minutes until loaves are lightly browned.

PIZZA DOUGH (*Makes one 12-inch round pizza*)

Preparation and Rising Time: 40 minutes
Baking Time: 10 minutes

½ cup hot tap water
1 tablespoon oil
2 teaspoons liquid barley
   malt

1½ cups All-Purpose Whole
   Wheat Bread Mix

In a bowl, combine water, oil and malt. Stir until malt is dissolved.

Stir in bread mix to form a soft dough.

Turn onto a floured board and knead for 10 minutes until smooth and elastic. Or knead in three batches in an electric food processor. If dough is sticky, knead in additional whole wheat flour.

Place ball of dough in a lightly oiled bowl and oil the top of dough. Cover with a warm, damp towel and allow to rise in a warm place for 30 minutes.

Preheat oven to 400 degrees.

Using moistened fingers, spread dough over a well-oiled pizza pan.

Bake for 5 minutes.

Remove from oven and top with sauce, cheese and other desired toppings. Bake for a final 5 minutes before serving.

WHOLE WHEAT CLOVER LEAF ROLLS (*Makes 12*)

Preparation and Rising Time: 2 hours
Baking Time: 20 minutes

1¾ cups scalded milk
½ cup liquid barley malt
⅓ cup melted butter

5 cups All-Purpose Whole
   Wheat Bread Mix
2 tablespoons sesame oil

In a bowl, combine hot milk, malt and butter. Stir until malt is dissolved.

Quickly stir in mix to form a soft dough. Turn onto a floured board and knead for 10 minutes until smooth and silky. Or knead in three small batches in an electric food processor. If dough is sticky, add additional flour as necessary but dough should remain pliable rather than stiff. Form into a ball and oil. Place in a bowl and cover with a warm, damp towel. Allow to rise in a warm place for 45 minutes until doubled in bulk. Punch down, and knead for 5 minutes.

Form into balls ½-inch in diameter. Place 3 balls in well-oiled muffin tins. Brush with sesame oil, cover and allow to rise for 50 minutes until doubled in bulk.

Preheat oven to 400 degrees.

Bake for 20 minutes until water sizzles when sprinkled on the bottom of the muffin tins and rolls slip easily out of tins.

WHOLE WHEAT BUTTERHORNS (Makes 24)

Preparation and Rising Time: 2½ hours
Baking Time: 20 minutes

1 cup scalded milk
3 tablespoons oil
⅓ cup liquid barley malt

3 eggs, beaten
5 cups All-Purpose Whole Wheat Bread Mix

¼ cup melted butter

In a bowl, mix milk, oil, malt and eggs until well combined. Quickly stir in bread mix to form a soft dough.

Turn onto a floured board and knead for 10 minutes until dough is smooth and elastic. Or knead in three small batches in an electric food processor. If dough is sticky, add more flour. However, dough should remain pliable rather than stiff.

Form into a ball and oil. Place in a bowl, cover with a damp, warm towel and allow to rise in a warm place for 45 minutes until doubled in bulk. Punch down and allow to rise a second time for 45 minutes.

Punch down again. Divide dough in two balls. On a floured board roll each ball into circles, 12 inches in diameter. Cut each circle in pie fashion to form 12 wedges in each circle. Brush each wedge with melted butter.

Roll each wedge, beginning at the outer edge and working toward the middle. Press the pointed end to secure.

Place rolls on well-oiled cookie sheet and brush with remaining melted butter. Cover and allow to rise in a warm place for 45 minutes until doubled.

Preheat oven to 400 degrees.

Bake for 20 minutes until lightly browned.

WHOLE WHEAT ENGLISH MUFFINS (*Makes 18*)

Preparation and Rising Time: 2 hours
Grilling Time: 30 minutes

2 cups scalded milk
2 tablespoons oil
2 tablespoons liquid barley malt

5 cups All-Purpose Whole Wheat Bread Mix
2 tablespoons cornmeal

In a bowl, combine milk, oil and malt until malt is dissolved.

Quickly stir in mix to form a dough. Turn onto a floured board and knead for 10 minutes until smooth and elastic. Or knead in three small batches in an electric food processor. If dough is sticky, knead in additional whole wheat flour as needed.

Form dough into a ball and oil. Place in a bowl and cover with a damp, warm towel. Allow to rise in a warm place for 1 hour until doubled in bulk.

Punch down. Form into a ball once again. Dust a board with cornmeal. Roll dough out on board to ¼-inch thickness. Cut into rounds, using a 3-inch cookie cutter, English muffin rings or empty tunafish tins.

When all dough is cut into rounds, place on a board and cover with a warm, damp towel. Allow to rise in a warm place for 45 minutes until doubled.

Heat a lightly oiled griddle or heavy frying pan to medium hot. Place muffins cornmeal side down on griddle and cook for 15 minutes. Turn over and cook for 15 minutes on the other side.

WHOLE WHEAT BAGELS (Makes 12 bagels)

Preparation and Rising Time: 1½ hours
Cooking Time: 45 minutes

1 cup hot tap water
2 tablespoons liquid barley malt
¼ cup oil

3 cups All-Purpose Whole Wheat Bread Mix
2 tablespoons blackstrap molasses

In a bowl, mix water, malt and oil until malt dissolves.

Beat in mix until a soft dough forms. Turn onto a floured board and knead for 10 minutes until smooth and elastic. Or knead in three small batches in an electric food processor. If dough is sticky, knead in whole wheat flour as necessary.

Form dough into a ball and oil. Place in a bowl and cover with a warm, damp towel. Allow to rise in a warm place for 45 minutes until doubled in bulk.

Punch down. Knead dough once again until smooth and elastic. Pull off pieces of dough and roll into ropes 6 inches by ¾-inch in diameter. Press ends of dough together to form a doughnut shape.

Place on a floured board, cover with a towel and allow to rise in a warm place for 15 minutes.

Preheat oven to 400 degrees.

Bring 2 quarts of water to a boil and stir in molasses. Drop bagels in boiling water 4 or 5 at a time. Wait 10 seconds, turn them over and wait another 10 seconds.

Remove them from water with a slatted spatula and place ½-inch apart on well-oiled cookie sheet. Continue boiling process until all bagels are on cookie sheets.

Bake for 25 minutes until golden brown.

ORANGE GLAZED ROLLS (*Makes 24*)

Preparation and Rising Time: 2 hours
Baking Time: 20 minutes

ROLL INGREDIENTS

1½ cups hot tap water	2 eggs, beaten
½ cup melted butter	5 cups All-Purpose Whole
⅓ cup liquid barley malt	Wheat Bread Mix

ORANGE BUTTER INGREDIENTS

4 tablespoons melted butter   1 tablespoon maple syrup
1 tablespoon finely grated orange peel

ORANGE GLAZE INGREDIENTS

¼ cup liquid barley malt   ¼ cup fresh orange juice
¼ cup non-instant powdered milk

DOUGH

To make dough, combine water, melted butter, malt and eggs in a bowl. Beat until well combined.

Quickly stir in mix. Turn onto a well-floured board and knead for 10 minutes until smooth and elastic. Or knead in three small batches in an electric food processor. If dough is sticky, knead in additional whole wheat flour. Dough should remain soft, however, and not become stiff.

Form into a ball and oil. Place in a bowl, cover with a warm, damp towel and allow to rise for 45 minutes until doubled in bulk.

ORANGE BUTTER

Beat together melted butter, maple syrup and orange peel near the end of the rising time.

Punch down dough and allow to stand 10 minutes.

On a floured board, roll dough into a rectangle 10 inches by 20 inches. Brush dough with orange butter. Cut dough into 1-inch strips 10 inches long. Place 5 strips on top of one another and cut each stack into 6 equal pieces.

Place each stack in generously oiled muffin tins. Cover with a towel and allow to rise in a warm place for 30 minutes until doubled in size.

Preheat oven to 400 degrees.

Bake for 20 minutes until lightly browned.

ORANGE GLAZE

While rolls bake prepare glaze. In a saucepan, heat malt, orange juice and milk powder over medium heat, stirring constantly for 7 minutes.

Remove rolls from oven and brush glaze on tops while still hot.

SOFT WHOLE WHEAT PRETZELS (Makes 12)

Preparation and Baking Time: 35 minutes

1½ cups hot tap water	5 cups All-Purpose Whole
2 tablespoons liquid barley	Wheat Bread Mix
malt	1 egg beaten with 1
2 eggs, beaten	teaspoon water
½ cup melted butter	2 tablespoons coarse salt

In a bowl, combine water, malt, eggs, and butter. Stir just until malt dissolves.

Quickly, beat in mix to form a soft dough. Turn onto a well-floured board and knead for 5 minutes until dough is smooth. Or knead in three small batches in an electric food processor. If dough is sticky, knead in whole wheat flour as necessary to make a soft but not stiff-textured dough.

Pull off pieces of dough and roll into ropes ½-inch in diameter and about 20 inches long. Make ropes into pretzel shapes on a well-oiled cookie sheet.

Preheat oven to 425 degrees.

Brush pretzels with egg-and-water mixture. Sprinkle with coarse salt.

Bake for 15 minutes until brown and crisp.

PECAN ROLLS *(Makes 12)*

Preparation and Rising Time: 2 hours
Baking Time: 35 minutes

DOUGH INGREDIENTS

2 cups scalded milk
2 tablespoons blackstrap
  molasses
¼ cup oil

1 teaspoon grated orange
  rind
⅔ cup raisins
3½ cups All-Purpose Whole
  Wheat Bread Mix

PECAN TWIST AND GLAZE INGREDIENTS

½ cup butter
¾ cup liquid barley malt

1½ cups chopped pecans
1 teaspoon coriander

DOUGH

In a bowl, beat milk, molasses and oil.

In a separate bowl, combine orange rind, raisins and bread mix.

Beat dry ingredients into liquid mixture to form a soft dough. Turn onto a well-floured board and knead for 10 minutes until smooth and elastic. Or knead in three small batches in an electric food processor. If dough is sticky, knead in whole wheat flour as necessary. Dough should not become stiff but remain pliable.

Form into a ball and oil. Place in a bowl and cover with a damp, warm towel. Allow to rise in a warm place for 1 hour until doubled in bulk. Punch down and divide into 2 pieces.

On a floured board roll each piece into a rectangle 6 inches by 12 inches. Cut each rectangle into 2-inch by 6-inch strips. Cover with a towel.

PECAN TWIST AND GLAZE

In a saucepan, melt butter. Stir in malt and cook until malt thins to a maple-syruplike consistency.

Drizzle ¾ cup of mixture over strips of dough. Sprinkle with 1 cup of pecans and with coriander.

Mix remaining ½ cup pecans into remaining ½ cup malt-and-butter mixture and set aside.

ASSEMBLING

Roll strips in jelly-roll fashion and place them in well-oiled muffin tins.

Drizzle remaining nut-and-malt glaze over tops of muffins.
Allow to rise in a warm place for 45 minutes, until doubled.
Preheat oven to 375 degrees.
Bake for 35 minutes until water sizzles when sprinkled on the bottom of muffin tins.

GERMAN PUFFS (*Makes 24*)

Preparation and Rising Time: 1 hour
Baking Time: 20 minutes

3 tablespoons liquid barley malt	1½ cups scalded milk
3 eggs, separated	2¼ cups All-Purpose Whole Wheat Bread Mix
3 tablespoons oil	¼ cup oil

In a bowl beat together malt, egg yolks, oil and scalded milk.

Using a wire whisk, beat in bread mix to form a batter.

Beat egg whites until stiff. Fold into batter.

Turn batter into a well-oiled bowl, cover with a damp towel, place in a pan of hot water and set in a warm place for 40 minutes.

Oil muffin tins generously and heat in a 400 degree oven. Remove tins from oven and spoon any remaining oil into each tin.

Spoon two generous tablespoons of batter into each muffin tin and bake at 400 degrees for 20 minutes.

YEAST WHOLE WHEAT DOUGHNUTS (*Makes 18*)

Preparation and Rising Time: 2 hours
Frying Time: 25 minutes

2 eggs, beaten	¾ cup hot tap water
2 tablespoons oil	2½ cups All-Purpose Whole
3 tablespoons liquid barley	Wheat Bread Mix
malt	Oil for deep frying

In a bowl, beat together eggs, oil, malt and hot water until malt dissolves.

Beat in bread mix to form a soft dough. Turn onto a well-floured board and knead for 10 minutes until smooth and elastic.

Form into a ball and oil. Place in a bowl, cover with a damp towel and allow to rise for 40 minutes.

Punch down and roll out dough on a lightly floured board to ½-inch thickness. Cut out doughnuts using a doughnut cutter.

Place rings on a lightly floured baking sheet 1½ inches apart. Cover with a towel and allow to rise in a warm place for 40 minutes until nearly doubled in bulk.

Heat 2 inches of oil in a heavy frying pan or deep frying utensil to 375 degrees.

Fry doughnuts several at a time until golden on one side and then turn until golden on the second side. Drain on paper towels.

BASIC RYE BREAD MIX
(*Makes 20 cups mix*)

9 cups rye flour	⅓ cup nutritional yeast
9 cups whole wheat flour	4 teaspoons salt or salt
8 tablespoons instant baking	substitute
yeast	

In a large bowl, combine all ingredients and mix thoroughly. Place in an airtight canister. Store in cool dry cupboard and use within one month or keep in refrigerator for two months for maximum nutritional value and to retain yeast's freshness.

CARAWAY RYE BREAD (*Makes 1 loaf*)

Preparation and Rising Time: 2 hours
Baking Time: 40 minutes

1¼ cups scalded milk
1 tablespoon blackstrap
   molasses

1 egg
½ tablespoon caraway seeds
5 cups Rye Bread Mix

In a bowl, beat milk, molasses and egg until well combined. In a separate bowl, mix caraway seeds and bread mix.

Beat dry mixture into liquid ingredients to form a dough. Turn onto a floured board and knead for 10 minutes until smooth and elastic. Or knead in three small batches in an electric food processor. If dough is sticky, knead in more flour. Texture of dough can be stiff.

Form into a ball and oil. Place in a bowl and cover with a warm, damp towel. Allow to stand in a warm place for 45 minutes until doubled in bulk. Punch down.

Form into a loaf and place in a well-oiled loaf pan. Cover and allow to rise for 45 minutes until doubled in bulk once again.

Preheat oven to 375 degrees.

Bake for 40 minutes until water sizzles when sprinkled on the bottom of the pan and until loaf slips easily from pan.

SWISS RYE BREAD (*Makes 1 loaf*)

Preparation and Rising Time: 2 hours
Baking Time: 1 hour

1¾ cups hot whey   5 cups Rye Bread Mix
2 tablespoons blackstrap
  molasses

In a bowl, mix hot whey and molasses. Beat in mix to form a dough.

Turn onto a well-floured board and knead for 10 minutes until smooth and elastic. Or knead in three small batches in an electric food processor. If dough is sticky, knead in just enough flour to prevent sticking.

Shape into a ball. Oil and place in a bowl, cover with a warm, damp towel and allow to rise in a warm place for 1 hour until doubled in bulk. Punch down.

Form into a round loaf and place on an oiled baking sheet. Oil loaf and set in a warm place to rise for 45 minutes.

Preheat oven to 325 degrees.

Bake for 1 hour or longer until loaf sounds hollow when knocked on with knuckles.

SWEDISH RYE BREAD (*Makes 1 loaf*)

Preparation and Rising Time: 2½ hours
Baking Time: 1 hour

1¾ cups hot tap water   1 tablespoon ground
3 tablespoons liquid barley   caraway seeds
  malt   1 tablespoon ground anise
2 tablespoons oil   seeds
1 tablespoon grated orange   1 tablespoon ground fennel
  rind   seeds
             5 cups Rye Bread Mix

In a bowl, mix hot water, malt and oil until malt dissolves.

In a separate bowl, combine orange rind, caraway, anise and fennel seeds and bread mix until well distributed.

Beat dry mixture into liquid ingredients to form a dough. Turn onto a well-floured board and knead for 10 minutes until smooth and elastic. Or knead in three small batches in an electric food processor. If dough is sticky, knead in enough flour to prevent sticking. Dough should be stiff enough to hold its own shape.

Form into a ball and oil. Place in a bowl and cover with a warm, damp towel. Allow to rise in a warm place for 45 minutes until doubled in bulk. Punch down and re-form into a ball. Allow to rise a second time for 45 minutes. Punch down.

Form into a round loaf, place on an oiled baking sheet and oil. Allow to rise in a warm place for 30 minutes.

Preheat oven to 300 degrees.

Bake for 1 hour until loaf sounds hollow when knocked upon with knuckles.

OLD TIME PUMPERNICKEL BREAD (*Makes 1 loaf*)

Preparation and Rising Time: 3 hours
Baking Time: 1½ hours

⅓ cup cornmeal	2 tablespoons oil
⅔ cup cold water	1 cup cooked pureed potatoes
⅔ cup boiling water	5 cups Rye Bread Mix
1 tablespoon blackstrap molasses	1 egg white, lightly beaten
	2 tablespoons sesame seeds

In a saucepan, mix cornmeal and cold water. Cook over high heat while gradually stirring in boiling water. When mixture thickens, remove from heat and stir in molasses, oil, and pureed potatoes.

Beat in bread mix to form a dough. Turn onto a floured board and knead for 10 minutes until smooth and elastic. Or knead in three small batches in an electric food processor. If dough is sticky, knead in additional rye flour to form a stiff dough.

Form a ball, oil and place in a bowl. Cover with a damp, warm towel and allow to rise for 1½ hours until doubled in bulk. Punch down.

Form into a loaf and place in a well-oiled loaf pan. Cover and allow to rise in a warm place for 1 hour until doubled in bulk.

Preheat oven to 375 degrees.

Brush loaf with egg white and sprinkle with sesame seeds.

Bake for 1½ hours until water sizzles when sprinkled on the bottom of the pan and loaf slips easily out of pan.

RYE BREAD STICKS (*Makes 24*)

Preparation and Rising Time: 30 minutes
Baking Time: 15 minutes

¾ cup hot tap water
1 tablespoon blackstrap
    molasses
2 cups Rye Bread Mix

1 egg, beaten
3 tablespoons coarse salt or
    sesame seeds

In a bowl, combine water and molasses. Stir in bread mix to form a soft dough.

Turn onto a floured board and knead for 10 minutes until smooth and elastic. Or knead in three small batches in an electric food processor. If dough is sticky, knead in enough flour to prevent sticking.

Divide dough into 25 pieces. Roll each piece into a rope ½-inch in diameter and 9 inches long. Place on an oiled baking sheet, cover and allow to stand in a warm place for 10 minutes.

Preheat oven to 425 degrees.

Brush sticks with beaten egg and sprinkle with salt or sesame seeds.

Bake for 15 minutes until browned.

BASIC OATMEAL WHEAT BREAD MIX
(Makes 20 cups mix)

9 cups oatmeal
9 cups whole wheat flour
1 cup non-instant powdered milk
¼ cup gluten flour

7 tablespoons instant baking yeast
½ cup nutritional yeast
1 tablespoon salt or salt substitute

In a large bowl, combine all ingredients and mix thoroughly. Place in an airtight canister. Store in cool dry cupboard or refrigerator and use within two months for maximum nutritional value and to retain yeast's freshness.

OATMEAL BREAD (Makes 1 loaf)

Preparation and Rising Time: 2 hours
Baking Time: 1¼ hours

2 cups scalded milk
⅓ cup liquid barley malt
2 tablespoons oil

5 cups Oatmeal Wheat Bread Mix

In a bowl, combine milk, malt and oil until malt is dissolved.

Beat in bread mix to form a soft dough. Turn onto a floured board and knead for 10 minutes until smooth and elastic. If dough is sticky, knead in enough additional flour to prevent sticking.

Form into a ball and oil. Place in a bowl and cover with a damp towel. Set in a warm place and allow to rise for 1 hour until soft and springy when touched lightly.

Punch down and knead for 5 minutes.

Form into a loaf and place in a well-oiled loaf pan. Cover and allow to rise in a warm place for 45 minutes until doubled in bulk.

Preheat oven to 300 degrees.

Bake for 1¼ hours until lightly browned and bread separates from sides of pan.

OATMEAL BATTER BREAD (Makes 1 loaf)

Preparation and Rising Time: 3 hours
Baking Time: 55 minutes

2½ cups scalded milk
⅓ cup liquid barley malt
2 tablespoons oil
¼ cup raisins

½ teaspoon cinnamon
5 cups Oatmeal Wheat
Bread Mix

In a bowl, combine milk, malt, oil, raisins and cinnamon.
Beat in bread mix to form a stiff batter. Set bowl in a warm
pan of water, cover with a towel and allow to rise in a warm
place for 1½ hours.

Stir with a wooden spoon to release air. Pour into a well-
oiled bread pan. Cover and allow to rise in a warm place for
45 minutes.

Place in a cold oven. Set heat to 375 degrees and bake for
15 minutes. Reduce heat to 325 and bake for 40 minutes
longer, until loaf is lightly browned and dough does not stick
to a toothpick when inserted.

DILL OATMEAL BREAD (Makes 1 loaf)

Preparation and Rising Time: 2 hours
Baking Time: 40 minutes

¼ cup chopped onion
½ cup boiling water
2 cups creamed cottage
cheese
2 eggs

2 tablespoons blackstrap
molasses
2 tablespoons dill seeds
4½ cups Oatmeal Wheat
Bread Mix

1 tablespoon butter

In an electric blender or food processor, combine onion,
boiling water, cottage cheese, eggs and molasses to form a
smooth mixture.

Turn into a bowl and mix in dill seeds and bread mix to
form a stiff batter. Cover and allow to stand in a warm place
for 1 hour until doubled in bulk. Stir to remove air.

Turn into a buttered casserole dish and allow to rise for 45 minutes in a warm place until doubled in bulk.
Preheat oven to 350 degrees.
Bake for 40 minutes until loaf sounds hollow when tapped.
Rub top with butter to soften crust.

RAISIN OATMEAL BREAD (Makes 1 loaf)

Preparation and Rising Time: 2 hours
Baking Time: 1¼ hours

2 cups scalded milk	1 teaspoon cinnamon
¼ cup liquid barley malt	1 cup raisins
1 egg	5 cups Oatmeal Wheat Bread
2 tablespoons oil	Mix

In a bowl beat together milk, malt, egg and oil until well combined.

In a separate bowl stir together cinnamon, raisins and bread mix.

Beat dry ingredients into liquid mixture to form a soft dough. Turn onto a floured board and knead for 10 minutes until smooth and elastic. Or knead in three small batches in an electric food processor. If dough is sticky, knead in just enough flour to prevent sticking.

Form into a ball, oil and place in a bowl. Cover with a damp, warm towel and set in a warm place to rise for 1 hour until doubled in bulk. Punch down.

Form into a loaf and place in a well-oiled loaf pan. Oil top and allow to rise in a warm place for 45 minutes until doubled in bulk.

Preheat oven to 350 degrees.
Bake for 1¼ hours until loaf sounds hollow when tapped.

OATMEAL MUFFINS (Makes 12)

Preparation and Rising Time: 2 hours
Baking Time: 20 minutes

1½ cups hot tap water	¼ cup liquid barley malt
2 tablespoons oil	Pinch nutmeg
3 cups Oatmeal Wheat Bread Mix	

In a bowl, beat together hot water, oil, malt and nutmeg. Stir in bread mix to form a stiff but sticky batter. Beat with a wooden spoon for 2 minutes.

Cover bowl with a damp, warm towel and allow to rise in a warm place for 1 hour until doubled in bulk.

Stir down batter and spoon into 12 well-oiled muffin tins. Set in a warm place and allow to rise 45 minutes.

Preheat oven to 400 degrees, and bake for 20 minutes until golden brown.

BASIC QUICK WHOLE WHEAT BREAD OR MUFFIN MIX

(Makes 20 cups mix)

9 cups whole wheat flour	1½ tablespoons salt or salt substitute
9 cups whole wheat pastry flour	1⅓ cups non-instant powdered milk
⅓ cup baking powder	
¼ cup baking soda	

In a large bowl, combine all ingredients and mix thoroughly. Place in an airtight canister. Store in cool dry cupboard and use within two months for maximum nutritional value.

QUICK WHOLE WHEAT LOAF (*Makes 1 loaf*)

Preparation and Baking Time: 55 minutes

2 eggs, beaten
2¼ cups water

2 tablespoons blackstrap
molasses
4 cups Quick Whole Wheat
Bread or Muffin Mix

Preheat oven to 350 degrees.

In a bowl, beat eggs, water and molasses. Stir in mix until thoroughly moistened.

Turn batter into a well-oiled loaf pan.

Bake at 350 degrees for 45 minutes, until water sizzles when sprinkled on the bottom of the pan.

QUICK WHOLE WHEAT RAISIN LOAF
(*Makes 1 loaf*)

Preparation and Baking Time: 55 minutes

2 eggs, beaten
2¼ cups water
1 teaspoon cinnamon

⅓ cup liquid barley malt
1 cup raisins
4 cups Quick Whole Wheat
Bread or Muffin Mix

Preheat oven to 350 degrees.

In a bowl, beat eggs, water, cinnamon and malt. Stir in raisins and gradually beat in mix.

Turn into a well-oiled loaf pan.

Bake at 350 degrees for 45 minutes, until water sizzles when sprinkled on the bottom of the pan.

BANANA BREAD (*Makes 1 loaf*)

Preparation and Baking Time: 1 hour

1 egg
¼ cup liquid barley
1½ cups sliced bananas

¼ cup yogurt or buttermilk
2 cups Quick Whole Wheat
Bread or Muffin Mix

Preheat oven to 350 degrees.
In an electric blender or food processor, puree egg, malt and bananas. Turn into a bowl. Stir in yogurt or buttermilk. Beat in mix with a wooden spoon.
Turn batter into a well-oiled loaf pan.
Bake for 50 minutes, until water sizzles when sprinkled on the bottom of the pan.

PUMPKIN BREAD (*Makes 1 loaf*)

Preparation and Baking Time: 1 hour, 5 minutes

1½ cups pureed pumpkin
2 tablespoons blackstrap molasses
2 tablespoons liquid barley malt

½ teaspoon cinnamon
2½ cups Quick Whole Wheat Bread or Muffin Mix

Preheat oven to 350 degrees.
In a bowl, mix pumpkin, molasses and malt until well combined. Stir in cinnamon and mix until thoroughly moistened.
Turn batter into a well-oiled loaf pan.
Bake for 55 minutes, until water sizzles when sprinkled on the bottom of the pan. Allow to cool before removing from pan.

DATE-NUT BREAD (*Makes 1 loaf*)

Preparation and Baking Time: 1 hour, 5 minutes

¾ cup dates
2 cups water
1 egg, beaten

1 cup coarsely chopped walnuts or pecans
2¼ cups Quick Whole Wheat Bread or Muffin Mix

In a saucepan, cook dates in water for 5 minutes until they form a sauce. Remove from heat and refrigerate until cool to lukewarm.

Preheat oven to 350 degrees.
Stir in egg and nuts to date mixture. Add bread mix until thoroughly moistened.
Turn into a well-oiled loaf pan.
Bake for 50 minutes, until water sizzles when sprinkled on the bottom of the pan.
Cool for 10 minutes before removing from pan.

NUT-BUTTER LOAF (Makes 1 loaf)

Preparation and Baking Time: 1 hour

¼ cup liquid barley malt	1 cup milk
⅔ cup peanut, almond or cashew butter	2¼ cups Quick Whole Wheat Bread or Muffin Mix

Preheat oven to 350 degrees.
In a blender or food processor, mix malt, nut butter and milk until smooth. Turn into a bowl and stir in bread mix.
Pour into a well-oiled loaf pan and bake for 50 minutes, until water sizzles when sprinkled on the bottom of the pan.

ORANGE-NUT LOAF (Makes 1 loaf)

Preparation and Baking Time: 1 hour

2½ cups milk	1 cup chopped walnuts
½ cup blackstrap molasses	2 tablespoons grated orange peel
⅓ cup oil	
4⅔ cups Quick Whole Wheat Bread or Muffin Mix	2 teaspoons cinnamon

Preheat oven to 350 degrees.
In a bowl combine milk, blackstrap molasses and oil.
In a separate bowl, combine bread mix, walnuts, orange peel and cinnamon.
Stir dry ingredients into liquid mixture and mix until well combined.

Turn into a well-oiled loaf pan and bake for 45 minutes, until water sizzles when sprinkled on the bottom of the pan.

CRANBERRY BREAD (*Makes 1 loaf*)

Preparation and Baking Time: 1 hour, 5 minutes

¼ cup fresh orange juice
¼ cup hot water
2 tablespoons oil
1¼ cups liquid barley malt
1 cup whole raw cranberries

1 cup chopped walnuts
1 teaspoon grated orange peel
3 cups Quick Whole Wheat Bread or Muffin Mix

Preheat oven to 325 degrees.

In a bowl, combine orange juice, hot water, oil and malt. Stir until well combined.

Add cranberries, walnuts and orange peel.

Stir in bread mix until all ingredients are well distributed. Turn into a well-oiled loaf pan and bake for 45 minutes, until water sizzles when sprinkled on the bottom of the pan. Allow to cool 10 minutes before removing from pan.

SIMPLE MUFFINS (*Makes 12*)

Preparation and Baking Time: 25 minutes

1 egg, beaten
1 cup milk

2 cups Quick Whole Wheat Bread or Muffin Mix

Preheat oven to 400 degrees.

In a bowl, beat egg and milk. Stir in mix until well combined.

Turn batter into well-oiled muffin tins and bake for 20 minutes until golden brown.

CIDER JELLY MUFFINS (Makes 12)

Preparation and Baking Time: 30 minutes

1 egg, beaten	2 cups Quick Whole Wheat
1 cup apple juice	Bread or Muffin Mix
2 tablespoons cider jelly	

Preheat oven to 400 degrees.

In a bowl, beat egg and apple juice. Stir in mix to form a batter.

Spoon well-oiled muffin tins half full of batter. Drop 1 teaspoon cider jelly in the middle of batter. Spoon remaining batter over jelly.

Bake for 20 minutes until golden brown.

PINEAPPLE MUFFINS (Makes 12)

Preparation and Baking Time: 30 minutes

2 eggs, beaten	2⅓ cups Quick Whole Wheat
⅓ cup milk	Bread or Muffin Mix
1 cup crushed pineapple with juice	

In a bowl, combine eggs, milk and pineapple. Stir in bread mix until thoroughly moistened.

Spoon into well-oiled muffin tins and bake for 20 minutes until golden brown.

CARAMEL-NUT MUFFINS (Makes 12)

Preparation and Baking Time: 35 minutes

6 tablespoons butter	2 eggs, beaten
6 tablespoons liquid barley malt	¾ cup milk
	¼ cup liquid barley malt
6 tablespoons chopped pecans or walnuts	2 cups Quick Whole Wheat Bread or Muffin Mix

Preheat oven to 400 degrees.

In a saucepan, melt butter. Stir in malt and cook for 5 minutes, stirring constantly. Remove from heat and mix in nuts.

Spoon 1½ tablespoons of malt mixture into each well-oiled muffin tin. Set aside.

In a separate bowl, beat eggs, milk and malt until combined. Stir in bread mix.

Spoon batter into muffin tins containing malt-nut mixture. Bake for 20 minutes until golden brown.

BLUEBERRY MUFFINS (Makes 12)

Preparation and Baking Time: 30 minutes

1 egg, beaten	2⅓ cups Quick Whole Wheat
1 cup milk	Bread or Muffin Mix
1 cup fresh blueberries	

Preheat oven to 400 degrees.

In a bowl, beat egg and milk together. Stir in blueberries. Gently stir in bread mix.

Spoon into well-oiled muffin tins and bake for 20 minutes until golden brown.

APPLE MUFFINS (Makes 12)

Preparation and Baking Time: 30 minutes

1 cup applesauce	½ cup chopped nuts
¼ cup apple juice	½ cup raisins
2 eggs, beaten	¼ teaspoon cinnamon
2½ cups Quick Whole Wheat Bread or Muffin Mix	

Preheat oven to 400 degrees.

In a bowl, beat together applesauce, apple juice and eggs.

In a separate bowl, mix nuts, raisins, cinnamon and bread mix.

Gradually stir dry ingredients into liquid mixture.

Pour into well-oiled muffin tins and bake for 20 minutes until golden brown.

WHOLE WHEAT DROP BISCUITS (*Makes 12*)

Preparation and Baking Time: 20 minutes

2 cups Quick Whole Wheat   ¼ cup melted butter or corn
   Bread or Muffin Mix   oil
                           ¾ cup milk

Preheat oven to 450 degrees.

In a bowl, combine mix and melted butter or oil with a fork until well distributed. Stir in milk.

Drop by tablespoons onto well-oiled cookie sheet. Bake for 10 minutes until golden brown.

ORANGE BISCUITS (*Makes 12*)

Preparation and Baking Time: 22 minutes

2 cups Quick Whole Wheat   ¼ cup orange juice
   Bread or Muffin Mix   ¼ cup milk
¼ cup melted butter or oil   ¼ cup liquid barley malt
1 tablespoon grated orange
   peel

Preheat oven to 450 degrees.

In a bowl, combine bread mix and butter or oil with a fork until well distributed. Stir in grated orange peel, orange juice, milk and malt until well combined.

Drop by tablespoons onto well-oiled baking sheet. Bake for 10 minutes until golden brown.

YOGURT BISCUITS (*Makes 12*)

Preparation and Baking Time: 15 minutes

2 cups Quick Whole Wheat   ¼ cup oil
  Bread or Muffin Mix   ¾ cup yogurt

Preheat oven to 450 degrees.

In a bowl, combine mix and oil until well distributed. Stir in yogurt.

Drop by tablespoons onto well-oiled baking sheet. Bake for 10 minutes until lightly browned.

CHEESE BISCUITS (*Makes 12*)

Preparation and Baking Time: 20 minutes

2 cups Quick Whole Wheat   ¼ cup melted butter or oil
  Bread or Muffin Mix   ¾ cup milk
         ⅓ cup grated Cheddar cheese

Preheat oven to 450 degrees.

In a bowl, combine mix and melted butter or oil until well distributed. Stir in milk and cheese.

Drop batter by tablespoons onto well-oiled baking sheet. Bake for 10 minutes until golden brown.

ROLLED BISCUITS (*Makes 12*)

Preparation and Baking Time: 30 minutes

2¼ cups Quick Whole Wheat   ¼ cup oil
  Bread or Muffin Mix   ¾ cup milk

Preheat oven to 450 degrees.

In a bowl, combine mix and oil with a fork until mixture resembles coarse cornmeal.

Stir in milk to form a dough which is soft but not sticky. Form into a ball.

On a well-floured board roll out dough ¾-inch thick and cut with a 2-inch biscuit cutter.

Place on well-oiled baking sheet and bake for 15 minutes until golden brown.

BASIC BRAN MUFFIN MIX
(Makes 20 cups mix)

9 cups bran	8 cups whole wheat flour
5 tablespoons low sodium baking powder	1½ teaspoons salt (optional)
	2⅔ cups raisins

In a large bowl, combine all ingredients and mix thoroughly. Place in an airtight canister. Store in cool dry cupboard and use within two months for maximum nutritional value.

BRAN MUFFINS (Makes 12)

Preparation and Baking Time: 30 minutes

1½ cups milk	3 tablespoons oil
1 egg, beaten	3 cups Bran Muffin Mix
3 tablespoons blackstrap molasses	

Preheat oven to 400 degrees.

In a bowl, beat together milk, egg, molasses and oil. Stir in mix until well combined.

Spoon into well-oiled muffin tins and bake for 20 minutes until browned.

YOGURT-BRAN MUFFINS (*Makes 12*)

Preparation and Baking Time: 30 minutes

1⅓ cups yogurt   ¼ cup blackstrap molasses
1 egg, beaten   3 tablespoons oil
                    3 cups Bran Muffin Mix

Preheat oven to 400 degrees.
In a bowl, beat together yogurt, egg, molasses and oil. Stir in mix until well moistened.
Spoon into well-oiled muffin tins and bake for 20 minutes until browned lightly.

APPLE-BRAN MUFFINS (*Makes 12*)

Preparation and Baking Time: 30 minutes

1⅓ cups apple juice or sweet   3 tablespoons oil
      cider   3 cups Bran Muffin Mix
2 eggs, beaten   1 cup dried chopped apples

Preheat oven to 400 degrees.
In a bowl, beat together apple juice, eggs and oil. Stir in mix until well moistened. Fold in apples.
Spoon into well-oiled muffin tins and bake for 25 minutes until lightly browned.

BANANA-BRAN MUFFINS (*Makes 12*)

Preparation and Baking Time: 30 minutes

2 eggs, beaten   ⅓ cup buttermilk
¼ cup liquid barley malt   2 tablespoons oil
1½ cups sliced bananas   3 cups Bran Muffin Mix

Preheat oven to 400 degrees.

In a blender or food processor, mix eggs, malt, bananas, buttermilk and oil until smooth. Turn into a bowl and stir in mix until moistened.

Spoon into well-oiled muffin tins and bake for 20 minutes until lightly browned.

BRAN DATE MUFFINS (Makes 12)

Preparation and Baking Time: 30 minutes

2 eggs, beaten	1 cup buttermilk
¼ cup liquid barley malt	⅔ cup chopped dates
3 cups Bran Muffin Mix	

Preheat oven to 400 degrees.

In a bowl, beat eggs, malt and buttermilk until well combined. Stir in dates and muffin mix until thoroughly moistened.

Turn into well-oiled muffin tins and bake for 20 minutes until lightly browned.

PUMPKIN-BRAN MUFFINS (Makes 12)

Preparation and Baking Time: 35 minutes

2 eggs, beaten	⅓ cup apple juice
¼ cup blackstrap molasses	2 tablespoons oil
1½ cups pureed pumpkin	3 cups Bran Muffin Mix

Preheat oven to 400 degrees.

In a bowl, beat together eggs, molasses, pumpkin, apple juice and oil. Stir in muffin mix until thoroughly moistened.

Spoon into well-oiled muffin tins and bake for 25 minutes until lightly browned.

BASIC CORNBREAD MIX
(*Makes 17 cups mix*)

9 cups cornmeal
6 cups whole wheat flour
1⅓ cups wheat germ
⅓ cup nutritional yeast
⅓ cup low sodium baking powder
2 teaspoons salt (optional)

In a large bowl, combine all ingredients and mix thoroughly. Place in an airtight canister. Store in cool dry cupboard and use within two months for maximum nutritional value.

CORNBREAD (*Makes one 8-inch square loaf*)

Preparation and Baking Time: 35 minutes

2 eggs, beaten
1 tablespoon oil
2 cups milk
2¾ cups Cornbread Mix

Preheat oven to 425 degrees.
In a bowl, beat eggs, oil and milk until well combined. Stir in cornbread mix until thoroughly moistened.
Pour into a well-oiled 8-inch square pan and bake for 25 minutes until water sizzles when sprinkled on the bottom of the pan.

CORN MUFFINS (*Makes 6*)

Preparation and Baking Time: 30 minutes

2 eggs, beaten
1 tablespoon oil
2 tablespoons blackstrap molasses
1¾ cups milk
2½ cups Cornbread Mix

Preheat oven to 425 degrees.
In a bowl, mix eggs, oil, molasses and milk until well combined. Stir in cornbread mix until thoroughly moistened.

Pour into well-oiled muffin tins. Bake for 20 minutes until a toothpick comes out clean when inserted into muffins.

SPOON BREAD (*Makes 1 loaf*)

Preparation and Baking Time: 1 hour, 25 minutes

2 cups scalded milk	2 tablespoons oil
1½ cups Cornbread Mix	3 eggs, separated
1 tablespoon blackstrap molasses	1 cup cold milk

In a saucepan, combine scalded milk and cornbread mix. Cook over medium heat, stirring constantly, until mixture thickens. Stir in molasses, oil and egg yolks. Remove from heat and stir in cold milk. Set aside.

Preheat oven to 350 degrees.

Beat egg whites until stiff and fold into cornmeal mixture. Pour into a well-oiled casserole dish and bake for 1 hour until golden brown.

CHILI CORNBREAD (*Makes one 8-inch square loaf*)

Preparation and Baking Time: 35 minutes

2 eggs, beaten	½ teaspoon chili powder
¼ cup chopped onion	¼ cup oil
¼ cup diced green peppers	¾ cup milk
2 tablespoons chopped jalapeño chili peppers	2½ cups Cornbread Mix

Preheat oven to 425 degrees.

In a bowl, combine eggs, onion, green peppers, chili peppers, chili powder, oil and milk. Stir until well combined. Stir in cornbread mix until thoroughly moistened.

Pour into a well-oiled 8-inch square baking pan. Bake for 20 minutes until golden brown.

BUTTERMILK CORNBREAD *(Makes 1 loaf)*

Preparation and Baking Time: 30 minutes

2 eggs, beaten
1 tablespoon oil
1¾ cups buttermilk

1 tablespoon blackstrap molasses
2½ cups Cornbread Mix

Preheat oven to 425 degrees.

In a bowl, beat together eggs, oil, buttermilk and molasses. Stir in cornbread mix until thoroughly moistened.

Pour into a well-oiled round 8-inch baking pan and bake for 20 minutes until golden brown.

CORN-SQUASH MUFFINS *(Makes 6)*

Preparation and Baking Time: 30 minutes

1 tablespoon oil
⅔ cup pureed winter squash

⅔ cup milk
3 cups Cornbread Mix

Preheat oven to 425 degrees.

In a bowl, combine oil, squash and milk. Stir in cornbread mix until thoroughly moistened.

Spoon into 6 well-oiled muffin tins and bake for 20 minutes until golden brown.

CORN CHEESE BREAD *(Makes one 8-inch square loaf)*

Preparation and Baking Time: 35 minutes

2 eggs, beaten
1 tablespoon oil

1¾ cups milk
2½ cups Cornbread Mix

1 cup grated Cheddar cheese

Preheat oven to 400 degrees.

In a bowl, beat together eggs, oil and milk. Stir in cornbread mix until thoroughly moistened. Fold in grated cheese.

Pour into a well-oiled 8-inch square pan and bake for 25 minutes until golden brown.

CHAPTER EIGHT

Cake and Cookie Mixes

It was only when we thought of combining whole wheat pastry flour with brown rice flour that we began to enjoy whole grain cakes in our home. Prior to that we had always found whole grain cakes heavy, more like hearty breads than light, fluffy cakes. Then, early in our experimentation for this book, we created the rice pancake mix. Much to our surprise, rice flour pancakes were as light in color and texture as their white flour counterparts.

We began using rice flour in cakes with similar results. Cakes, although still made only with whole grain flours, came out light, airy and moist. We recommend encouraging your local health food or natural food store manager to order brown rice flour, if he or she doesn't already have a supply in stock.

For very light cakes, stiffly beaten egg whites can be folded into the batter just before baking. However, many cakes can be made with the simple addition of liquid ingredients to a whole grain mix.

From only three basic cake mixes, you can make twenty-seven different cakes with a minimum of preparation.

As an alternative to sugar in baking, we do not recommend honey although it is widely used in other natural cookbooks. Honey is a very delicate and extremely sweet food. Although it contains valuable trace elements and enzymes in its raw form, these are destroyed when it is heated. Therefore, when cooked, honey has little more nutritional value than sugar and acquires many of sugar's negative characteristics. In fact, recent studies show that honey contributes as heavily and possibly more heavily to tooth decay than white sugar.

Instead of honey or sugar, we recommend the limited use of liquid barley malt, blackstrap molasses, date sugar, granulated maple sugar and apple juice. These sweeteners retain their nutritional integrity when cooked. For the most part, even these should be used only to enhance the natural sweet taste of foods instead of overpowering those tastes with their own flavor. You will quickly begin to wonder why conventional recipes require so much sugar or honey when you begin to taste the natural sweetness of grains, milk, dried milk powder, carob, raisins and dates.

Cookie mixes require less leavening than cake mixes since they are chewy or crisp rather than light and airy. They are also quicker and easier to make. Most of our dry mixes can be combined with liquids in one step and baked in under 18 minutes. The ease of preparation makes homemade mix cookies a perfect after-work-or-school treat.

BASIC CAKE MIX
(*Makes 18 cups mix*)

8 cups brown rice flour	1½ cups milk powder
8 cups whole wheat pastry flour	½ cup low sodium baking powder
1 teaspoon salt (optional)	

In a large bowl, mix all ingredients, using a wire whisk. When thoroughly distributed, spoon into an airtight canister. Store in cool dry cupboard and use within two months for maximum nutritional value.

VANILLA LAYER CAKE WITH CAROB FROSTING
(Makes one 2-layer cake)

Preparation and Baking Time: 45 minutes

CAKE INGREDIENTS

¼ cup butter   4 eggs, separated
¼ cup safflower oil   1½ cups milk
⅓ cup liquid barley malt   2 teaspoons vanilla
                    3½ cups Cake Mix

FROSTING INGREDIENTS

¼ cup butter   ¾ cup carob powder
                    ½ cup water

CAKE

Preheat oven to 375 degrees.

In a mixing bowl, cream together butter, oil and malt.

In a separate bowl, beat egg yolks, milk and vanilla. Set egg whites aside.

In a third bowl, sift mix.

Beat liquid ingredients and mix alternately into creamed butter and malt mixture, until combined to form a smooth batter.

Beat egg whites until stiff and fold into batter.

Pour into two well-oiled 8-inch-round baking pans and bake for 20 minutes until a toothpick comes out clean when inserted into the center of the cake.

FROSTING

While cake bakes, prepare frosting. Cream butter, carob powder and water together until smooth, using a blender or food processor.

Cool cake for 10 minutes before removing from pans, then frost with carob frosting.

CAROB CHIP CAKE (Makes one 2-layer cake)

Preparation Time: 20 minutes

¼ cup butter
¼ cup oil
⅓ cup liquid barley malt
4 eggs, separated

1½ cups milk
2 teaspoons vanilla
3½ cups Cake Mix
1½ cups carob chips

Preheat oven to 375 degrees.

In a mixing bowl, cream together butter, oil and malt.

In a separate bowl, beat egg yolks, milk and vanilla. Set egg whites aside.

In a third bowl, sift mix.

Beat liquid ingredients and cake mix alternately into creamed butter and malt until a smooth batter forms.

Stir in carob chips.

Beat egg whites until stiff and fold into batter.

Pour into two well-oiled 8-inch-round baking pans. Bake for 20 minutes until a toothpick comes out clean when inserted into the center of the cake.

Cool and frost with carob frosting as in the previous recipe.

FROSTED ORANGE CAKE (Makes one 2-layer cake)

Preparation and Baking Time: 45 minutes

CAKE INGREDIENTS

¼ cup butter
¼ cup oil
⅓ cup liquid barley malt
1 tablespoon grated orange
  rind

1½ cups milk
4 eggs, separated
3½ cups Cake Mix

FROSTING INGREDIENTS

1½ cups non-instant powdered
  milk

¼ cup butter
½ cup orange juice
1 tablespoon grated orange rind

CAKE

In a mixing bowl, cream butter, oil and malt. Stir in orange rind until well combined.

In a separate bowl, beat together milk and egg yolks. Set egg whites aside.

Sift mix in a separate bowl. Beat liquid ingredients and mix alternately into butter mixture to form a smooth batter.

Beat egg whites until stiff and fold into batter.

Pour into two well-oiled 8-inch-round cake pans and bake for 25 minutes until a toothpick comes out clean when inserted into the center of the cake.

Allow to cool for 10 minutes before removing from pans. Continue to cool on racks.

FROSTING

While cake cools, make frosting. In an electric blender or food processor beat together milk powder, butter, orange juice and grated orange rind until thick and smooth.

Frost cake when it is cooled.

COCONUT CAKE (*Makes one 2-layer cake*)

Preparation and Baking Time: 45 minutes

CAKE INGREDIENTS

¼ cup butter	4 eggs, separated
¼ cup safflower oil	1½ cups coconut milk or juice
⅓ cup liquid barley malt	3½ cups Cake Mix

FROSTING INGREDIENTS

1½ cups non-instant powdered milk	¼ cup butter
	½ cup coconut milk or juice
1 cup shredded unsweetened coconut	

CAKE

Preheat oven to 375 degrees.

In a mixing bowl, cream butter, oil and malt. In a separate bowl, mix egg yolks and coconut milk or juice. Set egg whites aside. Sift mix in a separate bowl.

Beat liquid ingredients and cake mix alternately into creamed butter-and-malt mixture to form a smooth batter.

Beat egg whites until stiff. Fold into batter.

Pour into two well-oiled 8-inch-round cake pans and bake for 25 minutes until a toothpick comes clean when inserted in center of cake.

Allow cakes to cool for 10 minutes before removing from pans. Cool on racks.

FROSTING

While cake cools, prepare frosting. In an electric blender or food processor beat powdered milk, butter and coconut milk or juice until smooth and thick.

Frost cake when cool and sprinkle with shredded coconut.

BOSTON CREAM PIE (*Makes 1 filled cake*)

Preparation and Baking Time: 40 minutes

CAKE INGREDIENTS

2 tablespoons butter	1 cup milk
2 tablespoons oil	1 teaspoon vanilla
3 tablespoons liquid barley malt	1¾ cups Cake Mix
	2 egg whites

CUSTARD FILLING

1 cup milk	2 egg yolks
1 tablespoon arrowroot starch dissolved in 2 tablespoons milk	1 teaspoon honey
	½ teaspoon vanilla

FROSTING INGREDIENTS

½ cup carob powder	2 tablespoons water
2 tablespoons liquid barley malt	

CAKE

Preheat oven to 375 degrees.

In a mixing bowl, cream butter, oil and malt. In a cup combine milk and vanilla.

Beat in liquid ingredients and cake mix alternately to creamed butter mixture to form a smooth batter.

Beat egg whites until stiff. Reserve yolks for custard filling. Fold whites into batter.

Pour half of batter into each of two well-oiled round 8-inch cake pans. Bake for 20 minutes until cake separates from sides of pans and cracks appear in the top of cakes.

CUSTARD AND FROSTING

While cake bakes, prepare custard and frosting.

To make custard, bring milk to a gentle boil in a heavy-bottomed saucepan. Stir in starch-and-milk mixture, and beat in egg yolks. Continue to stir until custard becomes smooth and thick, about three minutes.

Remove from heat and beat in honey and vanilla with a wire whisk. Set aside to cool.

To make frosting, beat carob powder, water and malt until smooth.

Remove cakes from oven and cool for 10 minutes. Remove from pans. Spread custard over first layer. Place second layer on top of custard and frost with carob frosting.

BANANA-NUT CAKE (*Makes one 2-layer cake*)

Preparation and Baking Time: 45 minutes

CAKE INGREDIENTS

¼ cup butter	1¼ cups pureed bananas
½ cup safflower oil	¾ cup chopped pecans or
¾ cup liquid barley malt	walnuts
3 eggs	3¼ cups Cake Mix
⅓ cup apple juice	

1½ cups non-instant powdered   ¼ cup butter
     milk   ½ cup water

CAKE

Preheat oven to 350 degrees.

In a bowl, cream butter, oil and malt until smooth. Beat in eggs one at a time. Stir in banana puree and nuts.

Mix in cake mix and stir in apple juice.

Pour batter into two oiled 8-inch-round cake pans. Bake for 30 minutes until a toothpick inserted into cake comes out clean.

Cool for 5 minutes before removing from pan. Cool completely on wire racks before frosting.

FROSTING

In an electric blender or food processor beat together milk powder, butter and water until smooth and thick. Frost cake immediately.

APPLE COFFEE CAKE (*Makes 1 cake*)

Preparation and Baking Time: 1 hour, 5 minutes

½ cup butter   ⅔ cup apple juice
⅓ cup liquid barley malt   2 cups thinly sliced, peeled
4 eggs   apples
3½ cups Cake Mix   1 tablespoon cinnamon

Preheat oven to 350 degrees.

Cream butter and malt. Beat in eggs one at a time. Stir in cake mix and apple juice to form a batter.

Pour one-third batter into a well-oiled 3-quart casserole. Spread half the sliced apples over batter and sprinkle with 1½ teaspoons cinnamon.

Spread one-third more batter over apples. Place remaining apples on this layer of batter and sprinkle with remaining cinnamon. Top with final third of batter.

Bake for 45 minutes. If cake becomes brown before cooking time has elapsed, cover with aluminum foil.

Serve from casserole while warm.

POUND CAKE (*Makes 1 loaf*)

Preparation and Baking Time: 1½ hours

1 cup butter	1 tablespoon grated lemon
½ cup maple syrup	rind
1 tablespoon lemon juice	4 eggs
1½ cups Cake Mix	

Preheat oven to 300 degrees.

Cream butter and maple syrup until smooth. Stir in lemon juice and rind.

Beat in eggs one at a time. Stir in mix until moistened.

Pour into a well-oiled loaf pan and bake for 1¼ hours, until edges are lightly browned and top is golden.

SPONGE CAKE WITH CAROB SAUCE
(*Makes 1 tube cake*)

Preparation and Baking Time: 55 minutes

CAKE INGREDIENTS

6 eggs, separated	⅓ cup apple juice
1⅓ cups Cake Mix	

SAUCE INGREDIENTS

¼ cup carob powder	¾ cup apple juice

CAKE

Preheat oven to 300 degrees.

Beat egg yolks until lemon colored. Stir in apple juice. Add cake mix and stir until well moistened.

Beat whites until stiff. Fold into batter. Pour into a well-oiled tube pan and bake for 40 minutes until golden.

Allow to cool 10 minutes before removing from pan.

SAUCE

Beat together carob powder and apple juice until smooth. Serve over cake hot or cold.

STRAWBERRY SHORTCAKE *(Serves 6)*

Preparation and Baking Time: 40 minutes

CAKE INGREDIENTS

4 eggs, separated   ⅓ cup apple juice
1 cup Cake Mix

TOPPING INGREDIENTS

1 quart sliced strawberries   2 teaspoons maple syrup or
honey
1 cup heavy cream, whipped

CAKE

Preheat oven to 300 degrees.

Beat egg yolks until lemon colored. Add apple juice. Stir in cake mix.

Beat whites until stiff. Fold into batter.

Pour into 12 well-oiled muffin tins. Bake for 20 minutes.

Allow to cool 10 minutes before removing from muffin tins.

TOPPING

While cakes cool, prepare topping. Mash sliced strawberries in maple syrup or honey with a potato masher until sauce forms.

Place two cakes on each plate and top with strawberry sauce and whipped cream.

BASIC GINGER AND SPICE CAKE MIX
(*Makes 18½ cups mix*)

8 cups whole wheat pastry flour	1½ cups non-instant powdered milk
8 cups brown rice flour	1 tablespoon ground cloves
½ cup non-alum baking powder	2 teaspoons ground allspice
1 tablespoon baking soda	4 tablespoons ground cinnamon
4 teaspoons ground ginger	1 teaspoon salt (optional)

In a large bowl, mix all ingredients, using a wire whisk. When thoroughly distributed, spoon into an airtight canister. Store in cool dry cupboard and use within two months for maximum nutritional value.

ENGLISH FRUIT CAKE (*Makes 1 loaf*)

Preparation and Baking Time: 1 hour, 20 minutes

½ cup safflower oil	¼ cup grape juice
⅓ cup liquid barley malt	1 cup raisins
4 eggs	½ cup chopped dates
1 tablespoon grated orange rind	½ cup dried, chopped apricots
1¼ cups Ginger and Spice Cake Mix	¾ cup walnuts

Preheat oven to 375 degrees.

Beat together oil and malt until well combined. Beat in eggs one at a time. Stir in orange rind and cake mix. Stir in grape juice.

Fold in raisins, dates, apricots and walnuts.

Pour into a well-oiled loaf pan and bake for 1 hour until cake separates from sides of pan and cracks down the middle. Cool for 10 minutes before removing from pan.

APPLESAUCE SPICE CAKE (*Makes 1 loaf*)

Preparation and Baking Time: 50 minutes

⅓ cup safflower oil	1 cup raisins or chopped
¼ cup liquid barley malt	dates
1 egg	1 cup thick applesauce
1⅔ cups Ginger and Spice Cake Mix	

Preheat oven to 350 degrees.

Beat together oil and malt until well combined. Beat in egg. Stir in mix, raisins or dates and applesauce.

Pour into a well-oiled loaf pan and bake for 40 minutes. Cool for 10 minutes before removing from pan.

CARROT FRUIT CAKE (*Makes 1 loaf*)

Preparation and Baking Time: 1 hour, 5 minutes

¼ cup oil	1½ cups Ginger and Spice
¼ cup liquid barley malt	Cake Mix
2 eggs	1 cup grated carrots
¾ cup apple juice	1 cup chopped dates

Preheat oven to 350 degrees.

Beat together oil, malt and eggs until well combined.

Stir in apple juice and cake mix alternately, a few table-spoons at a time, to form a batter.

Fold in carrots and dates.

Turn into a well-oiled loaf pan and bake for 45 minutes until golden brown. Allow to cool for 10 minutes before removing from pan.

FROSTED CARROT CAKE
(Makes one 9 × 13-inch sheet cake)

Preparation and Baking Time: 1¼ hours

CAKE INGREDIENTS

⅓ cup oil
⅓ cup liquid barley malt
4 eggs, beaten
2¼ cups Ginger and Spice Cake Mix

2 cups grated carrots
1½ cups raisins
1 cup walnuts

FROSTING INGREDIENTS

1½ cups non-instant powdered milk
¼ cup butter
½ cup water
½ teaspoon almond extract

CAKE

Preheat oven to 350 degrees.

Beat together oil, malt and eggs. Stir in cake mix, carrots, raisins and walnuts.

Pour batter into a well-oiled baking pan. Bake for 1 hour until cake separates from the sides of pan. Cool for 10 minutes before removing from pan.

FROSTING

In an electric blender or food processor beat together milk powder, butter, water and almond extract. Frost cake when cool.

SOUR CREAM SPICE CAKE
(Makes one 8 × 8-inch square cake)

Preparation and Baking Time: 55 minutes

CAKE

4 eggs, separated
⅓ cup apple juice
⅓ cup safflower oil
1 cup sour cream
2½ cups Ginger and Spice
Cake Mix
1 cup raisins

FROSTING

1½ cups non-instant powdered
milk
¼ cup butter
½ cup apple juice

CAKE

Preheat oven to 350 degrees.

Beat egg yolks until lemon colored. Stir in apple juice, oil and sour cream until smooth.

Stir in cake mix until well moistened. Add raisins.

Beat egg whites until stiff. Fold into batter.

Pour into a well-oiled baking pan and bake for 40 minutes until a toothpick inserted comes out clean.

Allow to cool for 10 minutes before removing from pan.

FROSTING

Beat together milk powder, butter and apple juice until smooth. Frost cake.

PEACH CAKE *(Makes one 10-inch round cake)*

Preparation and Baking Time: 1 hour, 20 minutes

CAKE INGREDIENTS

3 eggs, separated
½ cup oil
2 tablespoons maple syrup
2½ cups Ginger and Spice
Cake Mix
1 cup pear juice
1 cup diced peaches
1 cup shredded unsweetened coconut

FROSTING INGREDIENTS

1½ cups non-instant powdered   ½ cup pear or peach juice
   milk   2 peaches, cut in thin
¼ cup butter   wedges

CAKE

Preheat oven to 350 degrees.

Beat egg yolks until lemon-colored. Beat in oil and maple syrup.

Stir in cake mix and pear juice alternately to form a batter. Stir in peaches and coconut.

Beat egg whites until stiff. Fold into batter.

Pour into a well-oiled spring pan and bake for 1 hour until a toothpick inserted into the center of the cake comes out clean.

Allow to cool 10 minutes before removing from pan and frosting.

FROSTING

Beat milk powder, butter and juice until smooth. Frost cake and decorate with peach wedges.

SPICE CAKE (*Makes one 2-layered cake*)

Preparation and Baking Time: 50 minutes

CAKE INGREDIENTS

¼ cup butter   1½ cups apple juice or milk
¼ cup oil   3⅔ cups Ginger and Spice
⅓ cup liquid barley malt   Cake Mix
4 eggs, separated

FROSTING INGREDIENTS

2½ cups non-instant powdered   ¾ cup water
   milk   1 teaspoon cinnamon
½ cup butter   ⅔ cup chopped nuts

CAKE

Preheat oven to 375 degrees.

Cream butter, oil and malt until smooth and fluffy. Beat in egg yolks one at a time. Set aside egg whites.

Add apple juice or milk and cake mix alternately to butter, malt and egg mixture to form a batter.

Beat egg whites until stiff. Fold into batter.

Pour into two well-oiled 8-inch-round cake pans and bake for 30 minutes until a toothpick inserted into the center of the cake comes out clean. Allow to cool 10 minutes before removing cakes from pans.

FROSTING

In an electric blender or food processor, beat milk powder, butter, water and cinnamon until smooth.

Frost cake and sprinkle with nuts.

YAM CAKE (*Makes 1 tube cake*)

Preparation and Baking Time: 1 hour, 10 minutes

CAKE INGREDIENTS

½ cup oil
⅓ cup liquid barley malt
2 cups pureed yams
⅓ cup apple juice

3 eggs, separated
3 cups Ginger and Spice Cake Mix

GLAZE INGREDIENTS

1 cup non-instant powdered milk
3 tablespoons butter
⅔ cup water
½ teaspoon almond extract

CAKE

Preheat oven to 350 degrees.

Beat together oil and malt until well combined.

In a separate bowl, combine yam puree, apple juice and egg yolks.

Stir yam mixture and cake mix alternately into oil and malt mixture to form a batter.

Beat egg whites until stiff and fold into batter.

Pour into a well-oiled tube pan and bake for 50 minutes until a toothpick inserted into the cake comes out clean.

Allow to cool 10 minutes before removing from pan.

GLAZE

In an electric blender or food processor beat milk powder, butter, water and almond extract to form a thin frosting.

Pour glaze over cooled cake and allow to set until hard.

GINGERBREAD (*Makes one 9-inch square cake*)

Preparation and Baking Time: 1 hour, 5 minutes

¼ cup butter	¾ cup hot apple juice
¼ cup oil	2½ cups Ginger and Spice
½ cup blackstrap molasses	Cake Mix
2 eggs	1 cup raisins

1 cup heavy cream, whipped

Preheat oven to 350 degrees.

Cream butter, oil and molasses. Beat in eggs one at a time.

Add apple juice and cake mix alternately to butter mixture, a few tablespoons at a time, until a smooth batter is formed.

Stir in raisins.

Pour into a well-oiled baking pan. Bake for 45 minutes until a toothpick inserted into the center of the cake comes out clean.

Serve cut into squares and topped with whipped cream.

PINEAPPLE UPSIDE DOWN CAKE
(Makes one 9 × 13-inch cake)

Preparation and Baking Time: 1 hour

1 16-ounce can sliced pineapple, unsweetened
1 tablespoon arrowroot starch
¼ cup oil
¾ cup milk
⅓ cup liquid barley malt
2 eggs
2 cups Ginger and Spice Cake Mix

Arrange pineapple rings in the bottom of a buttered cake pan.

In a saucepan, bring juice from canned pineapple and starch to a gentle boil, stirring constantly. When mixture thickens pour over sliced pineapple and set pan aside.

In a bowl, beat oil and malt until well combined. Beat in eggs one at a time.

Add cake mix and milk alternately to egg mixture to form a smooth batter.

Pour over pineapple and bake for 40 minutes. Turn pan upside down over plate to remove, and cut into squares to serve.

BASIC CAROB CAKE MIX
(Makes 12 cups mix)

5½ cups roasted carob powder
3 cups whole wheat pastry flour
3 cups brown rice flour
¼ cup baking powder
¼ cup grain coffee

In a large bowl, mix all ingredients, using a wire whisk. When thoroughly distributed, spoon into an airtight canister. Store in cool dry cupboard and use within two months for maximum nutritional value.

SOUR CREAM CAROB CAKE *(Makes one 2-layer cake)*

Preparation and Baking Time: 50 minutes

CAKE INGREDIENTS

½ cup butter	½ cup apple juice
⅓ cup liquid barley malt	1 cup sour cream
4 eggs, separated	3 cups Carob Cake Mix

FROSTING

½ cup butter	1 cup water
1¼ cups carob powder	1 tablespoon grain coffee

CAKE

Preheat oven to 375 degrees.

Cream butter and malt. Beat in egg yolks one at a time, reserving egg whites.

In a separate bowl, mix apple juice and sour cream.

Add a few tablespoons of sour cream mixture and cake mix alternately to creamed mixture to form a smooth batter.

Beat egg whites until stiff. Fold into batter.

Pour into 2 well-oiled cake pans and bake for 30 minutes until a toothpick inserted into the center comes out clean.

Allow to cool for 10 minutes before removing from pans.

FROSTING

In an electric blender or food processor, beat butter, carob powder, water and grain coffee until smooth.

Frost cake when cool.

NUTTY CAROB CAKE *(Makes one 10-inch round cake)*

Preparation and Baking Time: 45 minutes

CAKE INGREDIENTS

¼ cup oil	½ cup hot apple juice
¼ cup melted butter	1 cup chopped walnuts or
1 cup milk	pecans
3 cups Carob Cake Mix	

FROSTING

½ cup non-instant powdered
milk
½ cup Carob powder
¼ cup butter

1 cup water
2 tablespoons liquid barley
malt

CAKE

Preheat oven to 350 degrees.

In a mixing bowl, mix oil, butter and milk. Beat in cake mix. Stir in apple juice and nuts.

Pour batter into a well-oiled cake pan and bake for 35 minutes until a toothpick comes out clean when inserted into the center of the cake.

Allow to cool 5 minutes before removing from pan.

FROSTING

In an electric blender or food processor beat milk powder, carob powder, butter, water and malt until smooth.

Frosting will be quite liquid. Spoon over cake as a glaze and allow to set.

ICE CREAM ROLL (*Makes one 9-inch roll*)

Preparation and Baking Time: 30 minutes
Freezing Time: 2 hours

5 eggs, separated
¼ cup liquid barley malt

1 cup Carob Cake Mix
2 tablespoons melted butter

2 cups honey ice cream

Preheat oven to 350 degrees.

Beat egg yolks and barley malt until well combined. Stir in mix to form a batter.

Beat egg whites until stiff. Fold into batter.

Butter an 18-inch long strip of wax paper and line a 9½ × 14-inch baking pan with it.

Pour batter into prepared pan and bake for 15 minutes until cake bounces back when pressed lightly with the fingertips.

Remove from oven and roll cake (along with wax paper) to form a 9½-inch roll.

Allow to cool for 15 minutes. Unroll and peel off paper carefully. Without pressing cake flat, spread ice cream over the inside of the roll. Reroll tightly and allow to freeze for 2 hours before serving.

CAROB CUPCAKES (*Makes 12*)

Preparation and Baking Time: 35 minutes

CUPCAKE INGREDIENTS

¼ cup butter	1 cup milk
¼ cup oil	1 egg
⅓ cup liquid barley malt	2 cups Carob Cake Mix

FROSTING INGREDIENTS

½ cup carob powder	¼ cup butter
	⅔ cup water

CUPCAKES

Preheat oven to 375 degrees.

Cream butter, oil and barley malt until smooth and well combined.

In a separate bowl, beat milk and egg until well combined.

Add a few tablespoons of milk-and-egg mixture and cake mix alternately to butter mixture to form a smooth batter.

Fill well-oiled muffin tins two-thirds full of batter.

Bake for 25 minutes until a toothpick inserted in cupcake comes out clean.

FROSTING

In an electric blender or food processor mix carob powder, butter and water until smooth.

Frost after cupcakes have cooled for 10 minutes.

CAROB PEANUT BUTTER BROWNIES (*Makes 16*)

Preparation and Baking Time: 35 minutes

¼ cup oil
¾ cup peanut butter
¼ cup liquid barley malt
2 tablespoons blackstrap
  molasses

2 eggs
¾ cup chopped prunes
⅓ cup Carob Cake Mix

Preheat oven to 350 degrees.

In a bowl, combine all ingredients in the above order. Mix well between each addition.

Pour into a well-oiled 9 × 9-inch square baking pan and bake for 25 minutes, until the surface is firm to touch. Cut into 16 pieces.

CAROB MINT CAKE (*Makes one 10-inch round cake*)

Preparation and Baking Time: 45 minutes

CAKE INGREDIENTS

¼ cup butter
¼ cup oil
⅓ cup liquid barley malt
4 eggs, separated

1¼ cups milk
3 cups Carob Cake Mix
1 teaspoon peppermint
  extract

FROSTING INGREDIENTS

¼ cup butter
½ cup water
¾ cup carob powder

½ teaspoon peppermint
  extract

CAKE

Preheat oven to 350 degrees.

Cream butter, oil and malt until light and fluffy. Beat in egg yolks. Set whites aside.

Alternately add a few tablespoons of milk and cake mix, mixing well to form a smooth cake batter. Stir in peppermint extract.

Pour batter into a well-oiled spring-form pan and bake for 30 minutes until a toothpick inserted into the center of the cake comes out clean.

FROSTING

In an electric blender or food processor, beat butter, water, carob powder and peppermint extract until smooth.

Cool cake for 5 minutes before removing from pan and frosting.

BASIC COOKIE MIX
(Makes 12¾ cups mix)

5 cups whole wheat pastry flour	5 cups raw wheat germ
3 tablespoons non-alum baking powder	2½ cups non-instant powdered milk
	1 teaspoon salt (optional)

In a bowl, mix all ingredients until well combined, using a wire whisk. Place in an airtight canister. Store in cool dry cupboard or in refrigerator. Use within two months for maximum nutritional value.

VANILLA COOKIES *(Makes 12)*

Preparation and Baking Time: 15 minutes

¼ cup safflower oil	1 egg
⅓ cup liquid barley malt	1 cup Cookie Mix
1 teaspoon vanilla extract	

Preheat oven to 350 degrees.

Using a wire whisk or food processor beat oil, malt and egg until well combined. Stir in cookie mix and vanilla.

Drop by spoonfuls onto well-oiled baking sheet. Bake for 10 minutes until edges are lightly browned.

CAROB COOKIES (*Makes 12*)

Preparation and Baking Time: 15 minutes

⅓ cup oil 1 egg
⅓ cup liquid barley malt ¾ cup Cookie Mix
⅓ cup roasted carob powder

Preheat oven to 350 degrees.
Using a wire whisk, electric beater or food processor, beat oil, malt and egg until well combined. In a separate bowl, mix cookie mix and carob powder. Stir dry mixture into liquid ingredients.
Drop batter by spoonfuls onto well-oiled baking sheet. Bake for 10 minutes.

CAROB CHIP COOKIES (*Makes 12*)

Preparation and Baking Time: 15 minutes

¼ cup oil 1 cup Cookie Mix
⅓ cup liquid barley malt 1 teaspoon vanilla extract
1 egg ½ cup carob chips

Preheat oven to 350 degrees.
Using a wire whisk, electric beater or food processor, beat oil, malt and egg until well combined. Stir in mix, vanilla and carob chips.
Drop by spoonfuls onto well-oiled baking sheet. Bake for 10 minutes.

PEANUT BUTTER COOKIES (*Makes 12*)

Preparation and Baking Time: 17 minutes

3 tablespoons oil 1 egg
3 tablespoons peanut butter ¼ cup liquid barley malt
1 cup Cookie Mix

Preheat oven to 350 degrees.

Using an electric blender, mixer or food processor, beat oil, peanut butter, egg and malt until smooth. Stir in cookie mix.

Drop by spoonfuls onto well-oiled baking sheet and bake for 10 minutes until edges are lightly browned.

PINEAPPLE MACAROONS (Makes 12)

Preparation and Baking Time: 17 minutes

4 egg yolks
2 tablespoons oil
¼ cup liquid barley malt
1 8½-ounce can drained
   crushed pineapple,
   unsweetened

½ cup Cookie Mix
⅔ cup shredded unsweetened
   coconut

Preheat oven to 350 degrees.

Using a wire whisk or food processor, mix egg yolks, oil and malt. Stir in crushed pineapple, cookie mix and coconut.

Drop by spoonfuls onto well-oiled baking sheet and bake for 12 minutes until edges are lightly browned.

DATE-FILLED DROP COOKIES (Makes 12)

Preparation and Baking Time: 20 minutes

DATE FILLING INGREDIENTS

½ cup chopped dates
3 tablespoons water

3 tablespoons chopped
   pecans or walnuts

COOKIE INGREDIENTS

¼ cup oil
⅓ cup liquid barley malt

1 egg
1¼ cups Cookie Mix

DATE FILLING

In a saucepan, combine dates and water. Cook for 5 minutes, stirring constantly, until mixture thickens. Stir in nuts and set aside.

COOKIES

Preheat oven to 350 degrees.

Using a wire whisk or a food processor, beat oil, malt and egg until well combined. Stir in cookie mix.

Drop cookie batter by spoonfuls onto well-oiled baking sheet. Make an impression in each cookie with a moistened thumb. Fill with ½-teaspoon date filling.

Bake for 10 minutes until lightly browned.

BUTTER COOKIES (*Makes 12*)

Preparation and Baking Time: 15 minutes

⅓ cup soft butter   ⅓ cup barley malt
1 cup Cookie Mix

Preheat oven to 350 degrees.

Using an electric beater or food processor, mix butter and malt until smooth. Stir in cookie mix.

Mixture should resemble dough. If necessary add slightly more mix or one tablespoon water.

Using moistened hands, shape into tablespoon-size balls. Place on well-oiled baking sheet and flatten with the bottom of a moistened glass. Bake for 10 minutes until edges are lightly browned.

SCONES (Makes 12)

Preparation and Baking Time: 30 minutes

2 cups Cookie Mix
⅓ cup butter
⅔ cup raisins

1 egg
¼ cup liquid barley malt
3 tablespoons yogurt

Preheat oven to 400 degress.

Using a pastry blender or a food processor, blend cookie mix and butter until mixture resembles coarse cornmeal. Stir in raisins.

Using a wire whisk or food processor, combine egg, malt and yogurt until smooth. Stir this mixture into cookie mix and butter mixture to form dough. Shape into a ball.

Roll out on a well-floured board to ¾-inch thick. Cut into diamond shapes by slicing diagonal lines across rolled-out dough. Place on well-oiled baking sheet and bake for 15 minutes until lightly browned.

LEMON COOKIES (Makes 12)

Preparation and Baking Time: 25 minutes

¼ cup oil
⅓ cup liquid barley malt
2 eggs, separated

1¼ cups Cookie Mix
2 teaspoons lemon juice
2 teaspoons grated lemon peel

Preheat oven to 325 degrees.

Using a wire whisk or a food processor, beat oil, malt and egg yolks until smooth. Set egg whites aside. Stir in cookie mix, lemon juice and lemon peel. Beat egg whites until stiff. Fold into batter.

Drop by spoonfuls onto well-oiled baking sheet and bake for 15 minutes until lightly browned. Allow to cool on a wire rack.

BASIC OATMEAL COOKIE MIX
(Makes 9½ cups mix)

5 cups rolled oats	1 cup raisins or currants
1 cup whole wheat pastry flour	2 tablespoons cinnamon
1 cup brown rice flour	2 tablespoons dried orange rind
½ cup raw wheat germ	2 tablespoons non-alum baking powder
½ cup non-instant powdered milk	

In a bowl, combine all ingredients and mix thoroughly with a wire whisk until well distributed. Place in an airtight canister. Store in cool dry cupboard and use within two months for maximum nutritional value.

OATMEAL COOKIES (*Makes 12*)

Preparation and Baking Time: 15 minutes

¼ cup oil	⅓ cup liquid barley malt
1 egg	1½ cups Oatmeal Cookie Mix

Preheat oven to 375 degrees.

Using a wire whisk or food processor, beat oil, egg and malt until well combined. Stir in mix. Drop by spoonfuls onto well-oiled baking sheet. Bake for 10 minutes.

CAROB OATMEAL COOKIES (*Makes 12*)

Preparation and Baking Time: 15 minutes

¼ cup oil	⅓ cup liquid barley malt
1 egg	1 cup Oatmeal Cookie Mix
⅓ cup roasted carob powder	

Preheat oven to 400 degrees.

Using a wire whisk or a food processor, beat oil, egg and malt until well combined. Stir in mix and carob powder. Drop by spoonfuls on well-oiled baking sheet and bake for 10 minutes until edges are lightly browned.

OATMEAL MACAROONS (Makes 20)

Preparation and Baking Time: 20 minutes

1 cup Oatmeal Cookie Mix	¼ cup apple juice
⅔ cup shredded unsweetened coconut	¼ cup liquid barley malt
	3 egg whites

Preheat oven to 350 degrees.

In a bowl, mix cookie mix and coconut. Stir in apple juice and malt. Beat egg whites until stiff. Fold into batter. Drop by spoonfuls onto well-oiled baking sheet and bake for 10 minutes until edges are lightly browned.

PEANUT BUTTER BARS (Makes 18)

Preparation and Baking Time: 30 minutes

DOUGH INGREDIENTS

⅓ cup butter	2 tablespoons liquid barley malt
1 egg	
5 tablespoons peanut butter	2 cups Oatmeal Cookie Mix

FROSTING INGREDIENTS

½ cup peanut butter	2 tablespoons liquid barley malt
3 tablespoons carob powder	

DOUGH

Preheat oven to 350 degrees.

Using an electric mixer or food processor, cream butter, egg, peanut butter and malt. Stir in cookie mix. Spread mixture in well-oiled 9 × 9-inch baking pan. Bake for 20 minutes until golden brown.

FROSTING

Cream peanut butter and malt until well combined. Stir in carob powder. Spread over cake while still warm. When cool cut into 18 bars.

CARROT OATMEAL COOKIES (*Makes 18*)

Preparation and Baking Time: 15 minutes

¼ cup oil
1 egg
¼ cup liquid barley malt

¼ cup milk
1⅔ cups Oatmeal Cookie Mix
½ cup grated carrot

Preheat oven to 400 degrees.

Using an electric mixer or food processor, beat oil, egg, malt and milk until well combined. Stir in mix and carrot. Drop by spoonfuls onto well-oiled baking sheet. Bake for 10 minutes until edges are lightly browned.

Cool on a rack before serving.

APPLESAUCE OATMEAL COOKIES (*Makes 24*)

Preparation and Baking Time: 25 minutes

¼ cup oil
2 tablespoons liquid barley malt

½ cup applesauce
2⅓ cups Oatmeal Cookie Mix

Preheat oven to 375 degrees.

Using a spoon, combine oil, malt and applesauce. Stir in mix. Drop batter by spoonfuls onto well-oiled baking sheet and bake for 20 minutes until lightly browned. Cool on a rack before serving.

CARAMEL CHIP OATMEAL BARS (Makes 24)

Preparation and Baking Time: 35 minutes

DOUGH INGREDIENTS

2 cups Oatmeal Cookie Mix   ⅔ cup butter

FILLING INGREDIENTS

⅔ cup liquid barley malt   ⅔ cup carob chips
1 cup non-instant powdered   ½ cup chopped walnuts or
   milk   pecans

DOUGH

Preheat oven to 350 degrees.

Using a pastry blender or food processor, combine cookie mix and butter. Press half mixture into well-oiled 9 × 13-inch baking pan.

Bake for 10 minutes until edges begin to brown.

FILLING

In a saucepan, heat malt until thin. Do not boil. Remove from heat and stir in milk powder.

Remove oatmeal crust from oven and sprinkle with carob chips and nuts. Drizzle with malt mixture.

Sprinkle remaining oatmeal dough over the top and bake for 10 minutes longer, until lightly browned.

Cut into bars.

BASIC SPICE COOKIE MIX
(Makes 12⅓ cups mix)

12 cups whole wheat pastry   2 tablespoons ground
   flour   cinnamon
1 tablespoon non-alum   1 tablespoon ground cloves
   baking powder   1½ teaspoons ground nutmeg
2 teaspoons baking soda   1½ teaspoons mace

In a large bowl, mix all ingredients until well combined, using a wire whisk. Place in an airtight canister. Store in cool dry cupboard and use within two months for maximum nutritional value.

SPICE CRISPS (*Makes 24*)

Preparation and Baking Time: 15 minutes

⅓ cup oil
⅓ cup liquid barley malt

⅓ cup yogurt
⅔ cup Spice Cookie Mix

Preheat oven to 350 degrees.
Beat together oil, malt and yogurt. Stir in mix until well combined.
Drop batter by spoonfuls onto well-oiled baking sheet. Bake for 10 minutes until edges are lightly browned. Cool on a rack.

JOE FROGGERS (*Makes ten 4-inch cookies*)

Preparation and Baking Time: 15 minutes
Chilling Time: 30 minutes

2 tablespoons hot water
3 tablespoons rum
¼ cup oil

¼ cup blackstrap molasses
¼ cup liquid barley malt
1 teaspoon ground ginger

2 cups Spice Cookie Mix

In a bowl, mix water, rum, oil, molasses, malt, ginger and cookie mix to form a cookie dough. Chill for 30 minutes.
Preheat oven to 375 degrees.
Shape dough into 10 round balls. Place 5 balls on each of two well-oiled baking sheets. Using the bottom of a floured glass, press each ball until it is 4 inches in diameter and ¼-inch thick.
Bake for 10 minutes.

SPICE SNAPS (Makes 12)

Preparation and Baking Time: 17 minutes
Chilling Time: 2 hours

¼ cup butter
⅓ cup blackstrap molasses
⅓ cup liquid barley malt
1 tablespoon grated orange
  peel

1 teaspoon orange juice
2¾ cups Spice Cookie Mix
12 pecan halves

In a bowl, mix butter, molasses, malt, orange peel and orange juice until well combined.

Stir in mix until thoroughly moistened. Chill for 2 hours or until desired use.

Preheat oven to 350 degrees.

Form dough into balls and place on a well-oiled baking sheet. Press a pecan half in center of each cookie.

Bake for 12 minutes and cool on a wire rack.

HERMITS (Makes 12)

Preparation and Baking Time: 22 minutes

¼ cup butter
⅓ cup blackstrap molasses
2 eggs, beaten

¼ cup milk
1⅓ cups Spice Cookie Mix
½ cup raisins

Preheat oven to 350 degrees.

Cream butter, molasses, eggs and milk until smooth and well combined. Stir in cookie mix and raisins.

Spread batter in well-oiled 11 × 14-inch baking pan. Bake for 12 minutes. Remove from oven and cut into squares.

CHRISTMAS DROP COOKIES (*Makes 24*)

Preparation and Baking Time: 20 minutes

⅓ cup butter
¼ cup maple syrup
2 eggs

1 teaspoon lemon juice
¾ cup Spice Cookie Mix
¼ cup currants or raisins

Preheat oven to 350 degrees.

Cream butter and maple syrup. Beat in eggs one at a time. Stir in cookie mix and currants or raisins.

Drop by spoonfuls about 3 inches apart on well-oiled or parchment-covered baking sheets.

Bake for 15 minutes and cool on a wire rack.

SPICE ICEBOX COOKIES (*Makes 24*)

Preparation and Baking Time: 20 minutes
Chilling Time: 3 hours (or longer)

2 cups Spice Cookie Mix   2 eggs, beaten

Place mix in a bowl. Pour in eggs and stir to form a dough.

Shape into a roll 2 inches in diameter. Cover with wax paper and place in refrigerator for at least three hours or until you wish to bake some fresh cookies.

Preheat oven to 375 degrees.

Cut roll into ⅛-inch slices and place on lightly oiled baking sheet. Bake for 10 minutes until edges are lightly browned.

You may use all or part of the roll. If only using part, the rest can be returned to the refrigerator for later use.

CARROT COOKIES (Makes 24)

Preparation and Baking Time: 25 minutes

¼ cup blackstrap molasses	½ cup cooked, mashed
¼ cup liquid barley malt	carrots
2 tablespoons oil	2¼ cups Spice Cookie Mix
1 cup chopped nuts	

Preheat oven to 350 degrees.

Blend molasses, malt and oil. Mix in carrots and cookie mix. Add nuts.

Drop by spoonfuls onto well-oiled baking sheet and bake for 15 minutes until lightly browned. Cool on a wire rack.

ROLLED SPICE COOKIES (Makes 30)

Preparation and Baking Time: 18 minutes
Chilling Time: 30 minutes

¼ cup blackstrap molasses	¼ cup oil
¼ cup liquid barley malt	2⅓ cups Spice Cookie Mix

Blend molasses, malt and oil. Stir in mix to form a stiff dough. Chill dough.

Preheat oven to 375 degrees.

On a floured board roll out dough 1/16-inch thin. Cut with cookie cutters and place on oiled baking sheet.

Bake for 8 minutes until edges are lightly browned. Allow to cool before serving.

CHAPTER NINE

Pie, Pudding and Frozen Dessert Mixes

As with cakes and cookies, the natural sweetness of the ingredients provides most of the flavor for pie crust and filling mixes and mixes for puddings, dried fruit and frozen desserts. A large variety of desserts can be created from a few handy mixes, with a minimum of time, planning and effort. We hope you enjoy these final sweet touches to a menu of mixes.

BASIC WHOLE WHEAT PIE CRUST MIX
(*Makes 5 cups mix*)

1¼ cups butter or oil	5 cups whole wheat pastry flour

In a bowl, work butter or oil into whole wheat pastry flour by rubbing between fingers until mixture resembles cornmeal. Spoon mixture into a wide-mouth jar. Store in the refrigerator for later use. This mix should be used within two weeks.

ROLLED PIE CRUST (Makes one 9-inch pie crust)

Preparation Time: 7 minutes
Bake according to individual pie recipes

1¼ cups Whole Wheat Pie   2 to 3 tablespoons ice water
Crust Mix

Measure mix into a bowl. Using a fork or food processor, mix water into mix until mixture adheres to itself to form a ball.

Place dough on a floured piece of waxed paper. Press dough with palm of hand and sprinkle with flour. Cover with a second piece of waxed paper and roll with a rolling pin until a circle 12 inches in diameter is formed.

Carefully peel off top piece of paper. Place 9-inch pie plate over dough, turn plate and dough with wax paper right side up. Remove paper at the same time fitting dough into pie plate.

Trim edges. Tuck under excess and pinch edges.

Bake according to individual recipes calling for a rolled pie shell.

If a double crust is required, double recipe and roll out two 12-inch circles. Line the pie plate with one as described and reserve the second for a top crust.

WHOLE WHEAT CRUMBLE TOPPING
(Makes 1¼ cups topping)

Preparation Time: None
Bake according to individual recipes

1¼ cups Whole Wheat Pie Crust Mix

Sprinkle mix directly over any fruit that has been prepared according to any crumble or crisp recipe and bake at 350 degrees for 30 minutes until topping is brown and crisp.

RICOTTA PIE CRUST (*Makes one 9-inch pie crust*)

Preparation Time: 5 minutes
Bake according to individual recipes

1¼ cups Whole Wheat Pie   ⅓ cup ricotta cheese
Crust Mix

Using a fork or food processor, stir pie crust mix and ricotta cheese together.
Press mixture into an oiled pie plate and bake according to any pressed crust pie recipe.

CHEDDAR CHEESE PIE CRUST
(*Makes one 9-inch pie crust*)

Preparation Time: 7 minutes
Bake according to individual recipes

1¼ cups Whole Wheat Pie   ⅓ cup grated Cheddar cheese
Crust Mix   2 to 3 tablespoons ice water

Using a fork, stir mix and grated cheese until evenly distributed. Stir in water 1 tablespoon at a time until dough adheres to itself and forms a ball.
If mix has not previously been refrigerated, chill for one hour. Otherwise dough may be rolled out on a floured board immediately.
Roll dough to form a 12-inch diameter circle and line an oiled pie plate. Trim edges and tuck under excess. Pinch around edge.
Bake according to recipes calling for rolled pie crusts.

SOUR CREAM PIE CRUST (*Makes one 9-inch pie crust*)

Preparation Time: 7 minutes
Bake according to individual recipes

1¼ cups Whole Wheat Pie   4 to 5 tablespoons sour cream
Crust Mix

Measure pie crust mix into a bowl. Using a fork or food processor, stir 1 tablespoon of sour cream into mix at a time until mixture adheres to itself. When dough is formed add no more sour cream.

If mix has not previously been refrigerated, chill for 30 minutes. If mix has been refrigerated dough can be rolled out directly.

Roll dough on a floured board to form a circle, 12 inches in diameter. Line a 9-inch pie plate. Trim edges and tuck excess under. Pinch around the edge of plate.

Bake according to recipes calling for a rolled pie crust.

EGG PASTRY (*Makes one 9-inch pie crust*)

Preparation Time: 7 minutes
Bake according to individual recipes

1¼ cups Whole Wheat Pie Crust Mix	1 egg
	2 teaspoons lemon juice
2 teaspoons water	

Place mix in a bowl. In a separate small bowl, beat egg, lemon juice and water.

Gradually stir liquid ingredients into mix to form a ball.

Roll dough on a floured board to form a circle, 12 inches in diameter. Line an oiled 9-inch pie plate and trim edges. Tuck under excess and pinch around the edge of the plate.

Bake according to recipes calling for rolled crusts.

BASIC COCONUT CRUMBLE OR CRUST MIX
(*Makes 8 cups mix*)

3 cups oatmeal	1 cup wheat germ
1 cup shredded unsweetened coconut	1 cup chopped nuts
	2 cups whole wheat flour

Blend oatmeal in an electric blender or food processor to form a coarse powder. In a large bowl, mix oatmeal powder with all other ingredients until thoroughly combined. Place in an airtight canister. Store in a cool dry cupboard and use within two months for maximum nutritional value.

COCONUT CRUMBLE (*Makes 1 cup topping*)

Preparation Time: 5 minutes
Bake according to individual recipes

1 cup Coconut Crumble or   ¼ cup softened butter
Crust Mix

Blend mix and butter with a pastry blender or food processor until mixture resembles coarse oatmeal.

Sprinkle mixture over apples, pears or other fruit that has been prepared according to any fruit crisp or crumble pie recipe.

COCONUT PIE CRUST (*Makes 1 pie shell*)

Preparation Time: 5 minutes
Bake according to individual pie recipes

¼ cup butter   1¼ cups Coconut Crumble or
3 tablespoons water   Crust Mix

Blend butter and mix with a pastry blender or food processor until mixture resembles coarse oatmeal.

Sprinkle with water and mix well.

Press mixture into a well-oiled pie plate and bake according to individual pie recipes calling for pressed pie shells.

BASIC WHEAT GERM CRUMBLE MIX
(*Makes 6 cups mix*)

3 cups wheat germ	1 cup chopped nuts
2 cups whole wheat flour	1½ cups butter or oil

In a bowl, combine wheat germ, flour and nuts until well distributed. Using fingers, rub in butter or oil until mixture resembles cornmeal. Place mixture in a tightly covered wide-mouth jar. Store in the refrigerator and use within two weeks.

WHEAT GERM CRUMBLE (*Makes 1 cup topping*)

Preparation Time: None
Bake according to individual recipes

1 cup Wheat Germ Crumble Mix

Sprinkle wheat germ crumble on top of any fruit prepared according to a crisp or crumble recipe.
Bake for the prescribed amount of time.

WHEAT GERM PIE CRUST (*Makes one 9-inch pie crust*)

Preparation Time: 5 minutes
Bake according to individual pie recipes

1¼ cups Wheat Germ Crumble Mix	2 to 3 tablespoons water

Mix crumble mix and water until evenly moistened. Press mixture into an oiled 9-inch pie plate and bake according to recipes calling for pressed pie crusts.

BASIC CAROB PUDDING MIX
(Makes 4 cups mix)

1⅓ cups carob powder
1⅔ cups non-instant powdered
 milk
⅔ cup arrowroot starch
¼ cup grain coffee

2 teaspoons ground
 cardamom
2 teaspoons ground
 cinnamon

In a large bowl, combine all ingredients and mix until thoroughly distributed. Spoon into a wide-mouth jar and seal tightly. Store in dry cool cupboard and use within two months for assurance of freshness.

CAROB PUDDING *(Serves 4)*

Preparation Time: 12 minutes

2 cups hot milk   1 cup cold milk
          1 cup Carob Pudding Mix

In a heavy saucepan, scald 2 cups milk and allow to remain on burner, reducing heat to medium low.

Mix cold milk and pudding mix until completely dissolved. Stir into cooking milk.

Cook, stirring constantly, for 5 minutes until pudding thickens. Remove from heat.

This pudding may be served hot or cold.

CAROB CREAM PIE *(Makes one 9-inch pie)*

Preparation Time: 20 minutes

1 pressed pie crust, Coconut
 Pie Crust (p. 209) or
 Wheat Germ Pie Crust
 (p. 210)

½ cup cold milk
¾ cup Carob Pudding Mix
1⅓ cups hot milk
1 cup heavy cream, whipped

Prepare pressed pie crust and bake at 350 degrees for 15 minutes until lightly browned. Remove from oven and allow to cool while preparing filling.

Beat together cold milk and pudding mix until smooth. In a saucepan, heat 1⅓ cups milk until scalded. Stir in cold milk and pudding mixture.

Cook over medium heat, stirring constantly for 5 minutes until pudding thickens. Remove from heat and pour into pie shell.

Allow to cool and top with whipped cream just before serving.

RUM CAROB CREAM PIE (*Makes one 9-inch pie*)

Preparation Time: 25 minutes

1 pressed pie crust, Coconut
     Pie Crust (p. 209) or
     Wheat Germ Pie Crust
     (p. 210)
	½ cup cold milk
	¾ cup Carob Pudding Mix
	1⅓ cups hot milk
	2 teaspoons rum

1 cup heavy cream, whipped

Prepare pressed pie crust and bake at 350 degrees for 10 minutes until lightly browned. Remove from oven and allow to cool while preparing filling.

Beat together cold milk and pudding mix until smooth. In a saucepan, heat 1⅓ cups milk until scalded. Stir in cold milk and pudding mixture.

Cook over medium heat, stirring constantly, for 5 minutes until mixture thickens. Remove from heat and stir in rum.

Pour into pie shell and allow to cool. Top with whipped cream just before serving.

CAROB CAKE PUDDING (Makes one 9 × 13-inch cake)

Preparation and Baking Time: 55 minutes

⅔ cup Carob Pudding Mix   ¼ cup oil
½ cup cold milk   ⅓ cup liquid barley malt
1 cup hot milk   1 cup cold milk
       1¾ cups Carob Cake Mix (p. 187)

Preheat oven to 375 degrees.

Beat together pudding mix and cold milk until smooth. Heat 1 cup hot milk to scalding and stir into pudding and cold milk mixture. Stir for 5 minutes until mixture thickens. Spread in the bottom of oiled baking pan.

In a bowl, mix oil, malt and cold milk. Stir in carob cake mix to form a smooth batter. Pour over the pudding.

Bake for 40 minutes until cake is firm. This dessert can be served hot or chilled.

CAROB COCONUT PUDDING OR PIE FILLING
(Serves 4)

Preparation Time: 12 minutes

1 cup Carob Pudding Mix   2 cups hot milk
¾ cup cold milk   ½ cup shredded unsweetened
                                      coconut

Combine pudding mix and cold milk until mix is dissolved. Heat the hot milk in a saucepan to a gentle boil. Reduce heat and stir in mix and milk combination. Stir for 5 minutes until thick and smooth. Stir in coconut.

This dessert can be served as a pudding or used to fill any baked pie crust.

CAROB SHERBET (*Serves 4*)

Preparation Time: 10 minutes
Freezing Time: 3 hours

1 cup Carob Pudding Mix   ¾ cup cold milk
2¼ cups hot milk

Beat pudding mix and cold milk until mix is dissolved. Heat 2¼ cups of hot milk in a saucepan until it begins to boil. Reduce heat and stir in pudding and milk mixture. Stir for 5 minutes until mixture thickens. Allow to cool.

Place in a covered, sturdy plastic container and freeze for 1 hour until mixture becomes mushy but not solid.

Beat with a rotary beater or fork until smooth.

Return to the freezer for another hour. Beat again until smooth. Return to the freezer, covered, for a final hour of freezing or until serving time.

CAROB ICE CREAM STICKS (*Makes 8 "popsicles"*)

Preparation Time: 12 minutes
Freezing Time: 2 hours

⅔ cup Carob Pudding Mix   ½ cup cold milk
1½ cups hot milk

Dissolve pudding mix in cold milk. Heat 1½ cups hot milk to a gentle boil. Reduce heat. Stir in pudding mix and cold milk combination. Stir for 5 minutes until mixture thickens.

Pour into a freezer tray and allow to set for 1 hour until mushy but not hard. Beat with a fork or rotary beater until smooth. Spoon mixture into a commercial "popsicle" maker and return to freezer.

These stick puddings may be served after an hour or as desired.

CAROB MOUSSE (Serves 6)

Preparation Time: 12 minutes
Freezing Time: 3 hours

1 cup Carob Pudding Mix   2¼ cups hot milk
¾ cup cold milk   1 cup heavy cream, whipped

Dissolve pudding mix in cold milk. Heat 2¼ cups milk to boiling. Reduce heat and stir in mix and cold milk mixture. Stir constantly for 5 minutes until thickened. Remove from heat and cool.

Fold in whipped cream and spoon into individual soufflé dishes. Allow to set for at least 3 hours in a freezer.

Before serving allow to soften at room temperature for 5 minutes.

BASIC PUDDING MIX
(*Makes 5 cups mix*)

2 cups arrowroot starch   1 cup granulated maple sugar
              2 cups non-instant powdered milk

In a bowl, combine all ingredients and mix until thoroughly distributed. Spoon into a wide-mouth jar and seal tightly. Store in cool dry cupboard and use within two months for assurance of freshness.

VANILLA PUDDING (Serves 4)

Preparation Time: 10 minutes

½ cup Pudding Mix   2⅔ cups hot milk
⅓ cup cold milk   1 teaspoon vanilla

Dissolve pudding mix in cold milk. Heat 2⅔ cups hot milk in saucepan until it boils gently. Reduce heat and stir in pudding and cold milk mixture. Stir for 5 minutes until thickened. Remove from heat and stir in vanilla.

VANILLA CREAM PIE *(Makes one 9-inch pie)*

Preparation Time: 25 minutes

1 pressed pie crust, Coconut Pie Crust (p. 209) or Wheat Germ Pie Crust (p. 210)	⅓ cup Pudding Mix
	⅓ cup cold milk
	1⅓ cups hot milk
	1 teaspoon vanilla

1 cup heavy cream, whipped

Prepare pressed pie crust and bake at 350 degrees for 10 minutes until lightly browned. Remove from oven and allow to cool while preparing filling.

Dissolve pudding mix in cold milk. In saucepan heat 1⅓ cups hot milk to boiling. Reduce heat and stir in pudding mix and milk combination. Stir for 5 minutes until thickened.

Pour into pie shell and allow to cool. Top with whipped cream just before serving.

BANANA PUDDING OR PIE FILLING *(Serves 4)*

Preparation Time: 12 minutes

½ cup Pudding Mix	2⅔ cups hot milk
⅓ cup cold milk	2 bananas, sliced

1 teaspoon pineapple juice

Dissolve pudding mix in cold milk. Heat 2⅔ cups hot milk to boiling. Reduce heat and stir in pudding mix and cold milk combination. Stir for 5 minutes until mixture thickens.

Toss sliced bananas in pineapple juice to prevent discoloring. Stir into pudding.

This dessert can be served directly as a pudding or used to fill any baked pie shell.

STRAWBERRY CREAM PIE (*Makes one 9-inch pie*)

Preparation Time: 25 minutes

1 pressed pie crust, Coconut Pie Crust (p. 209) or Wheat Germ Pie Crust (p. 210)	½ cup Pudding Mix ⅓ cup cold milk 1⅓ cups hot milk 1 cup sliced strawberries

1 cup heavy cream, whipped

Prepare pressed pie shell and bake at 350 degrees for 10 minutes until lightly browned. Remove from oven and allow to cool while preparing filling.

Dissolve pudding mix in cold milk. Heat 1⅓ cups hot milk to boiling. Reduce heat and stir in mix and milk combination. Stir for 5 minutes until mixture is smooth and thick.

Puree ¼ cup strawberries in an electric blender or food processor. Stir into pudding and remove from heat. Fold in remaining ¾ cup strawberries and pour into pie shell. Allow to cool.

Top with whipped cream just before serving.

BANANA MOUSSE (*Serves 6*)

Preparation Time: 15 minutes
Freezing Time: 3 hours

⅓ cup Pudding Mix ⅓ cup cold milk 1⅓ cups hot milk	3 bananas mashed with 3 tablespoons pineapple juice

1½ cups heavy cream, whipped

Dissolve pudding mix in cold milk. Heat 1⅓ cups hot milk in a saucepan to boiling. Reduce heat and stir in mix and milk combination. Stir for 5 minutes until thickened.

Remove from heat and stir in mashed bananas and pineapple juice combination. Allow to cool.

Fold in whipped cream. Spoon into individual soufflé dishes and freeze for 3 hours or longer.

Allow to soften at room temperature for 5 minutes before serving.

FROZEN VANILLA STICKS (Makes 8 "popsicles")

Preparation Time: 12 minutes
Freezing Time: 2 hours

⅓ cup Pudding Mix   1⅓ cups hot milk
⅓ cup cold milk   1 teaspoon vanilla

Dissolve mix in cold milk. Heat 1⅓ cups hot milk to boiling. Reduce heat. Stir in mix and milk combination. Stir for 5 minutes until thickened. Stir in vanilla.

Place in a freezer tray for 1 hour until mushy but not solid. Beat with a fork or rotary beater until smooth.

Spoon into a commercial "popsicle" maker and allow to freeze for one hour or longer until set.

PINEAPPLE CREAM PUDDING OR PIE FILLING (Serves 4)

Preparation Time: 12 minutes

½ cup Pudding Mix   1 cup drained crushed
½ cup cold milk   pineapple, unsweetened
2 cups hot milk

Dissolve pudding mix in cold milk. Heat 2 cups hot milk to boiling. Reduce heat. Stir in pudding mix and milk combination. Stir for 5 minutes until thickened.

Remove from heat and add pineapple.

This dessert can be served as a pudding or used to fill any baked pie shell.

COCONUT PUDDING OR PIE FILLING (Serves 4)

Preparation Time: 10 minutes

½ cup Pudding Mix
½ cup cold milk
2½ cups hot milk

⅔ cups shredded unsweet-
ened coconut
½ teaspoon almond extract

Dissolve pudding mix in cold milk. Heat 2½ cups hot milk to boiling. Reduce heat and stir in mix and milk combination. Stir in coconut and continue stirring for 5 minutes until pudding thickens.

Remove from heat and stir in almond extract.

This dessert can be served immediately as a pudding or used to fill any baked pie shell.

COFFEE PUDDING (Serves 4)

Preparation Time: 10 minutes

½ cup Pudding Mix
½ cup cold milk

2½ cups hot milk
1 tablespoon grain coffee

Dissolve pudding mix in cold milk. Heat 2½ cups hot milk to boiling. Reduce heat. Stir in mix and milk combination and grain coffee. Continue stirring constantly for 5 minutes until thickened.

Remove from heat and serve hot or cold.

COFFEE CREAM GELATIN (Serves 4)

Preparation Time: 20 minutes
Chilling Time: 2 hours

1 tablespoon agar agar
powder
2½ cups water

1½ tablespoons grain coffee
¼ cup Pudding Mix
dissolved in ¼ cup milk

¼ cup heavy cream

In a saucepan, sprinkle agar agar powder over water. Bring to a boil. Add grain coffee. Allow to boil for 5 minutes until agar agar is dissolved.

Stir in pudding mix and milk combination. Stir constantly for 5 minutes. Remove from heat and add heavy cream.

Pour into a gelatin mold or dish and allow to set in the refrigerator for 2 hours.

BASIC MINCEMEAT MIX
(Makes 6⅔ cups mix)

3 cups raisins	3 tablespoons dried orange
3 cups finely chopped dried	peel
apples	2 teaspoons cinnamon
⅓ cup arrowroot starch	2 teaspoons nutmeg

2 teaspoons cloves

In a bowl, combine all ingredients until evenly coated with starch. Spoon into a wide-mouth jar and seal tightly. Store in cool dry cupboard and shake well before each use. This mix will remain fresh for two months.

MINCEMEAT *(Serves 4)*

Preparation Time: 15 minutes

2 cups Mincemeat Mix   1 cup apple juice

In a saucepan, combine mix and apple juice. Cook for 10 minutes over medium-high heat, stirring occasionally until apples are tender and sauce has formed.

MINCEMEAT PIE *(Makes one 9-inch pie)*

Preparation and Baking Time: 45 minutes

1 unbaked rolled pie crust from Whole Wheat Pie Crust Mix (p. 210)	1 cup apple juice 3⅓ cups Mincemeat Mix

Preheat oven to 400 degrees.

Prepare pie crust.

In a saucepan, combine apple juice and mix. Bring to a boil, stirring occasionally. Pour into pie shell.

Bake for 30 minutes and cool before serving.

MINCEMEAT TAHINI PUDDING *(Serves 4)*

Preparation Time: 15 minutes

2 cups Mincemeat Mix	1 cup apple juice or cider

2 tablespoons tahini mixed with 2 tablespoons
water until smooth

In a saucepan, combine mix and apple juice or cider. Cook over medium-high heat, stirring occasionally, for 10 minutes until apples are tender and sauce has formed.

Remove from heat and stir in tahini-and-water mixture until well combined. Serve either hot or cold.

JELLED MINCEMEAT *(Serves 4)*

Preparation Time: 15 minutes
Jelling Time: 2 hours

2 cups apple juice or cider	1⅓ cups Mincemeat Mix

2 teaspoons agar agar powder

In a saucepan, combine apple juice or cider with mix. Sprinkle agar agar over mixture.

Bring to a gentle boil, stirring occasionally, for 10 minutes until agar agar dissolves and juice thickens slightly.

Pour into a gelatin mold or bowl, and refrigerate for 2 hours until firm.

BAKED MINCEMEAT CUSTARD (Serves 6)

Preparation and Baking Time: 50 minutes

¼ cup liquid barley malt
3 eggs, beaten
1 teaspoon soy flour

2 cups scalded milk cooled
  to lukewarm
1 cup Mincemeat Mix

Preheat oven to 350 degrees.

Combine all ingredients and turn into oiled custard cups or a soufflé dish.

Place cups or dish in a pan of hot water and bake for 45 minutes until firm. Serve hot or cold.

MINCEMEAT CRUMBLE (Makes one 9-inch pie)

Preparation and Baking Time: 45 minutes

3⅓ cups Mincemeat Mix
1 cup apple juice or cider

1 cup crumble topping,
  Coconut Crumble
  (p. 209), Whole Wheat
  Crumble (p. 206) or
  Wheat Germ Crumble
  (p. 210)

Preheat oven to 400 degrees.

In a pie plate or casserole dish combine mix and apple juice or cider until thoroughly moistened.

Sprinkle with crumble topping and bake for 40 minutes until golden brown and crisp.

BASIC DRIED FRUIT COMPOTE MIX
(*Makes 6⅓ cups mix*)

1 cup pitted prunes	1 cup dried apples
1 cup raisins	1 cup dried apricots
1 cup dried pears	1 cup dried peaches

⅓ cup arrowroot starch

In a large bowl, combine all ingredients until evenly coated with starch. Spoon into a wide-mouth jar and seal tightly. Store in cool dry cupboard and use within two months for maximum freshness.

COMPOTE (*Serves 4*)

Preparation Time: 15 minutes

2⅓ cups Dried Fruit Compote   1½ cups apple juice
Mix

In a saucepan, combine mix and apple juice. Cook over medium-high heat, stirring occasionally, for 15 minutes until fruit is soft and juice has thickened.

This dessert can be served hot or cold.

SWEDISH FRUIT SOUP (*Serves 4*)

Preparation Time: 20 minutes

2⅓ cups Dried Fruit Compote Mix	1 orange, cut in half and thinly sliced
2 cups apple juice	½ lemon, thinly sliced

1 teaspoon cinnamon

In a saucepan, combine all ingredients. Cook over medium-high heat for 15 minutes until fruit is soft and sauce has formed.

JELLED COMPOTE (Serves 4)

Preparation Time: 15 minutes
Jelling Time: 2 hours

2⅓ cups Dried Fruit
Compote Mix
2 cups apple juice

2 teaspoons agar agar
powder

In a saucepan, combine mix with apple juice. Sprinkle over agar agar. Bring to a gentle boil. Allow to boil, stirring occasionally, until agar agar dissolves.

Pour in a gelatin mold or bowl, and refrigerate for two hours, until firm.

DRIED FRUIT PIE (Makes one 9-inch pie)

Preparation and Baking Time: 45 minutes

3 cups Dried Fruit Compote
Mix
⅓ cup apple juice

1 unbaked pie shell (rolled
or pressed) (p. 206)

Preheat oven to 400 degrees.

Toss mix with apple juice until thoroughly moistened.

Turn into a prepared pie shell and bake for 40 minutes until shell is lightly browned.

DRIED FRUIT CRISP (Serves 4)

Preparation and Baking Time: 45 minutes

3 cups Dried Fruit Compote
Mix
1 cup apple juice

1 cup crumble topping,
Coconut Crumble (p. 209),
Whole Wheat Crumble
(p. 206) or Wheat Germ
Crumble (p. 210)

Preheat oven to 400 degrees.

Combine mix and apple juice and place in a pie plate or casserole dish. Sprinkle with crumble topping.

Bake for 40 minutes until topping is crisp and golden brown.

DRIED FRUIT PUREE *(Serves 4)*

Preparation Time: 20 minutes

2⅓ cups Dried Fruit Compote Mix	1 cup apple juice

In a saucepan, combine mix and juice. Cook over medium-high heat, stirring occasionally, for 15 minutes until fruit has softened.

Puree in an electric blender or food processor until smooth. Serve alone or as a topping for puddings or cakes.

BAKED FRUIT AND CAKE DESSERT *(Serves 6)*

Preparation and Baking Time: 55 minutes

2⅓ cups Dried Fruit Compote Mix	⅓ cup apple juice Spice Cake batter (p. 184)

Preheat oven to 350 degrees.

Toss fruit mix with apple juice and spread over the bottom of an oiled casserole dish.

Prepare batter and spread over dried fruit. Bake for 35 minutes until cake springs back when pressed lightly.

Spoon directly from casserole to serve either hot or cold.

MIXED FRUIT CHIFFON PIE (Makes one 9-inch pie)

Preparation Time: 30 minutes
Chilling Time: 2 hours

1 pressed pie shell, Coconut Pie Crust (p. 209), or Wheat Germ Pie Crust (p. 210)
2 cups Dried Fruit Compote Mix

1 cup apple juice
2 teaspoons agar agar powder
5 eggs, separated

Preheat oven to 350 degrees.

Bake pie crust for 10 minutes until lightly browned. Set aside to cool while preparing filling.

Combine compote mix and apple juice in a saucepan. Sprinkle with agar agar. Boil for 15 minutes until agar agar is dissolved and fruit is soft. Remove from heat and puree in an electric blender or food processor until smooth. Stir in egg yolks. Allow to cool.

Beat whites until stiff but not dry. Fold whites into puree.

Turn into pie shell and chill for 2 hours or longer before serving.

BASIC SWEET AND NUTTY RICE DESSERT MIX
(Makes 6 pint jars)

8 cups brown rice or basmati rice
2 cups raisins

30 cardamom pods
1½ cups chopped almonds

Pour 1⅓ cups rice in 6 pint jars. Place the seeds of 5 cardamom pods in each jar. Spoon ¼ cup nuts into each jar. Top each jar with ⅓ cup raisins. Seal jars tightly and store in cool dry cupboard. Use within four months for maximum flavor.

HEARTY RICE PUDDING (Serves 6)

Preparation Time: 4 hours

1 jar Sweet and Nutty Rice
Dessert Mix

1½ cups water
5 cups milk

In a covered pot, boil rice mix and water for 10 minutes. Reduce heat to medium low and add milk. Cook uncovered for several hours until pudding is thick and creamy.

SWEET RICE DESSERT (Serves 4)

Preparation Time: 1½ hours

1 jar Sweet and Nutty Rice
Dessert Mix

4 cups apple juice or cider

In a covered pot, bring rice mix and apple juice or cider to a boil. Reduce heat to simmer and cook, covered, until soft.

ORANGE SWEET RICE DESSERT (Serves 4)

Preparation Time: 1 hour

2⅓ cups water
1 jar Sweet and Nutty Rice
Dessert Mix
⅔ cup fresh orange juice

1 tablespoon grated orange
rind
2 oranges, sectioned, with
membranes removed

In a covered pot, bring water and rice mix to a boil. Reduce heat to low and cook for 40 minutes until tender.

Stir in orange juice, orange rind and orange sections. Cook, covered, for 15 more minutes before serving.

PEACHY 'N NUTTY RICE DESSERT (Serves 4)

Preparation Time: 1 hour

3 cups water	½ cup pureed peaches
1 jar Sweet and Nutty Rice Dessert Mix	2 peaches, sliced

In a covered pot, bring water and rice mix to a boil. Reduce heat to low and cook for 45 minutes until tender.

Stir in peach puree and peach slices and cook for 10 minutes before serving.

APPLE NUT RICE DESSERT (Serves 4)

Preparation Time: 1 hour

3½ cups apple juice	2 teaspoons cinnamon
1 jar Sweet and Nutty Rice Dessert Mix	2 apples, finely chopped

In a covered pot, bring apple juice and rice mix to a boil. Reduce heat to low and cook for 40 minutes until rice is tender.

Stir in cinnamon and apples. Cook for 15 minutes before serving.

BAKED RICE DESSERT (Serves 6)

Preparation Time: 5 minutes
Baking Time: 4 hours

6 cups milk	1 jar Sweet and Nutty Rice Dessert Mix
½ cup chopped dates	

Preheat oven to 300 degrees.

Place milk, dates and rice mix in a 2-quart casserole or baking dish. Stir well.

Bake for 1 hour until a light brown skin forms. Stir in skin. Continue baking for 30 minutes and stir in a second skin. Check every 30 minutes for the first 3 hours of baking and stir in skin.

Allow to bake for a final hour until top is well browned and dessert is thick and creamy.

PINEAPPLE RICE PUDDING (Serves 4)

Preparation Time: 1 hour

3 cups water
1 jar Sweet and Nutty Rice Dessert Mix

1 cup crushed pineapple, unsweetened
1 cup heavy cream, whipped

In a covered pot, bring water and rice mix to a boil. Reduce heat and cook, covered, for 40 minutes until tender.

Stir in pineapple and cook for 15 minutes.

Serve hot or cold, topped with whipped cream.

FLUFFY RICE PUDDING (Serves 4)

Preparation Time: 1¼ hours
Chilling Time: 30 minutes

1½ cups water
1 jar Sweet and Nutty Rice Dessert Mix

2 cups milk
2 eggs, separated

In a covered pot, bring water and rice mix to a boil. Boil 5 minutes. Reduce heat to medium and add milk. Cook for 50 minutes uncovered, until thick and creamy.

Stir in egg yolks. Remove from heat and allow to cool.

Beat egg whites until stiff. Fold into cooled pudding. Chill and serve cold.

RICE RING (Serves 4)

Preparation Time: 1 hour
Baking Time: 30 minutes

1½ cups water	2 cups milk
1 jar Sweet and Nutty Rice	3 eggs, beaten
Dessert Mix	3 eggs, separated

In a covered pot, bring water and rice mix to a boil. Reduce heat to medium and add milk. Cook, uncovered, for 45 minutes until rice is tender and thick. Remove from heat and allow to cool.

Stir in beaten eggs and egg yolks. Beat whites until stiff and fold into mixture.

Preheat oven to 350 degrees.

Pour into a well-oiled ring mold and bake for 30 minutes until firm.

Remove from mold and serve on a large platter.

JELLED RICE (Serves 6)

Preparation Time: 1 hour
Jelling Time: 2 hours

2¾ cups water	1 tablespoon agar agar
1 jar Sweet and Nutty Rice	powder
Dessert Mix	⅔ cup fresh strawberries or
2 cups apple juice	blueberries
½ cup yogurt or sour cream	

In a covered pot, bring water and rice mix to a boil. Reduce heat to medium low and cook, covered, for 40 minutes until rice is soft.

In a separate saucepan, measure apple juice, and sprinkle with agar agar powder. Bring to a boil. Boil for 5 minutes until agar agar is completely dissolved.

In a large bowl, combine cooked rice mix, apple juice, berries and yogurt or sour cream. Pour into a gelatin mold or bowl and allow to set for two hours until firm.

Glossary

agar agar is a sea gelatin. It is available at health food stores, but can be replaced by one envelope of unflavored gelatin if not easily obtained.

basmati rice is a naturally white grain that cooks in 20 minutes and has the appearance of white refined rice while retaining all the nutrition of a whole grain.

garam masala is a curry spice found in Indian specialty shops, natural food stores and specialty shops. If not available, ordinary curry powder may be substituted.

hiziki seaweed is a mild seaweed that is shaped like thin threads. It is black in color and expands when moisture is added to it. Hiziki is available at most natural food stores.

miso is a dark paste made from soybeans and grain which are fermented with salt. The high salt content and the formentation enable it to be stored without refrigeration. It is a common product readily available at health and natural food stores.

soba is Japanese buckwheat spaghetti. It cooks very quickly and has a delicate buckwheat flavor. It is available in the specialty sections of many supermarkets and in health and natural food stores.

tahini is a seed butter made from sesame seeds. It is a common Middle Eastern food and can be readily found at specialty shops and in health and natural food stores.

Index

ABC soup mix, basic, 45
  ABC soup, 46
    bean, 47
    cream of, 46
    non-dairy, 47
    tamari broth, 46
Acorn squash, Navy bean stuffed, 81
Additives, 7
Agar agar, 231
  coffee cream gelatin, 219–20
  jellied compote, 224
  jellied mincemeat, 221–22
  jellied rice, 230
  mixed fruit chiffon pie, 226
Anemia, 8
Almond(s):
  basic sweet and nutty rice
      dessert mix, 226
  apple nut rice dessert, 228
  baked rice dessert, 228–29
  fluffy rice pudding, 229
  hearty rice pudding, 227
  jellied rice, 230
  orange sweet rice dessert, 227
  peach 'n nutty rice dessert, 228
  pineapple rice pudding, 229
  rice ring, 230
  sweet rice dessert, 227
  butter:
    rice nut pancakes, 21
    nut-, loaf, 158
  curried rice with, 118
Apple(s):
  applesauce:
    oatmeal cookies, 199
    and sour cream buckwheat
        pancakes, 16
    spice cake, 181
  buckwheat pancakes, 16
    applesauce and sour cream, 16
  coffee cake, 177–78
  griddle cakes, rice, 21
  jellied mincemeat, 221–22
  malted, cracked wheat cereal, 27

millet porridge, 29
muffins, 161–62
  -bran, 165
nut rice dessert, 228
raisin coconut oatmeal, 24
Apple juice as sweetener, 171
Arteriosclerosis, 4
Avocado dressing, 63

Bagels, whole wheat, 142
Banana:
  bread, 156–57
  -bran muffins, 165–66
  mousse, 217–18
  -nut cake, 176–77
  pudding or pie filling, 216–17
Barbecue Shake and Bake, 8
Barley malt, 14, 171
  basic malted cracked wheat
      cereal mix, 26
    cracked wheat breakfast
        loaf, 27–28
    cracked wheat cream cereal, 26
    malted apple cracked wheat
        cereal, 27
    malted cracked wheat cereal, 26
    morning wheat cookies, 27
  sweet wheat puffs, 33–34
  wheat cakes, 32–33
Beans and bean mixes, 75–113
  ABC soup, 47
  black-eyed pea mix, basic
      Southern, 76
  Boston bean mix, basic, 80
  chick-pea mix:
    basic curried, 91
    Middle East style, basic, 95
  dark variety bean mix, basic, 84
  kidney bean mix, basic, 103
  lentil mix, basic European, 99
  pinto bean mix, basic Mexican, 109
  split green pea mix, basic, 87
  see also specific mixes
Beet dressing, 64

Biscuits:
  cheese, 163
  orange, 162
  rolled, 163–64
  whole wheat drop, 162
  yogurt, 163
Basmati rice, 231
  see also Rice
Black-eyed pea mix, basic
  Southern, 76
  black-eyed pea:
    and corn cobbler, 78
    pie, 77–78
    stuffed peppers, 78
    and tomato dinner, 79
  Southern hopping John, 76–77
Blackstrap molasses, 14, 171
  pancakes, rice, 20
  wheat germ, raisins and nut
    cereal, 33
Blueberry(ies):
  buckwheat pancakes, 17
  jellied rice, 230
  muffins, 161
Blue cheese dressing, 64
Boston bean mix, basic, 80
  Boston bean(s), 80–81
    with fruit, 82
    Navy bean stuffed acorn
      squash, 81
    sweet and sour, stew, 83
    turnovers, 81
Boston cream pie, 175–76
Bottles and jars, 9–10
Brain damage and MSG, 7
Bran:
  basic, muffin mix, 164
    apple-bran muffins, 165
    banana-bran muffins, 165–66
    bran date muffins, 166
    bran muffins, 164
    pumpkin-bran muffins, 166
    yogurt-bran muffins, 165
  flakes, 30
Bread and yeast mixes, quick, 131–69
  bran muffin mix, basic, 164
  cornbread mix, basic, 167
  oatmeal wheat bread mix,
    basic, 152
  rye bread mix, basic, 147–48
  whole wheat bread mix, basic
    all-purpose, 132
  whole wheat bread or muffin
    mix, basic quick, 155
  see also specific mixes
Breakfast corn raisin muffins, 19
Breakfast bars, oatmeal, 25
Breakfast loaf, cracked wheat,
  27–28
Breakfast mixes, 13–34
  bran flakes, 30
  buckwheat pancake mix, basic,
    14–15

coconut raisin granola, 32
corn wheat griddle cake mix,
  basic, 17
malted cracked wheat cereal
  mix, basic, 26
malted wheat cakes, 32–33
molasses, wheat germ, raisins
  and nut cereal, 33
raisin coconut oatmeal mix,
  basic, 23
rice griddle cake mix, basic, 19–20
sesame buckwheat granola, 31–32
spiced millet porridge mix,
  basic, 28
sweet wheat puffs, 33–34
variety flake granola, 31
see also specific mixes
Breakfast patties, millet, 30
Broth. *See* Dark broth mix, basic;
  Herb broth mix, basic
Brown gravy:
  dark, 54
  light, 54–55
  onion, 40
Brownies, carob peanut butter, 191
Brown rice. *See* Rice
Brown rice flour, 170
  basic cake mix, 171
    apple coffee cake, 177–78
    banana-nut cake, 176–77
    Boston cream pie, 175–76
    carob chip cake, 173
    coconut coconut cake, 174–75
    frosted orange cake, 173–74
    pound cake, 178
    sponge cake with carob
      sauce, 178–79
    strawberry shortcake, 179–80
    vanilla layer cake with
      carob frosting, 172
  basic carob cake mix, 187
    carob cupcakes, 190
    carob mint cake, 191–92
    carob peanut butter
      brownies, 191
    ice cream roll, 189–90
    nutty carob cake, 188–89
    sour cream carob cake, 188
  basic ginger and spice cake
    mix, 180
    applesauce spice cake, 181
    carrot fruit cake, 181–82
    English fruit cake, 180–81
    frosted carrot cake, 182
    gingerbread, 186
    peach cake, 183–84
    pineapple upside down cake, 187
    sour cream spice cake, 183
    spice cake, 184–85
    yam cake, 185–86
  basic oatmeal cookie mix, 197
    applesauce oatmeal cookies, 199
    caramel chip oatmeal bars, 200

carob oatmeal cookies, 197–98
carrot oatmeal cookies, 199
oatmeal cookies, 197
oatmeal macaroons, 198
peanut butter bars, 198–99
basic rice griddle cake mix, 19–20
rice apple griddle cakes, 21
rice flour morning cake, 22
rice flour pancakes, 20
rice molasses pancakes, 20
rice nut butter pancakes, 21
Buckwheat:
groats. *See* Kasha
pancake(s), 15
apple, 16
applesauce and sour cream, 16
blueberry, 17
buttermilk, 15
mix, basic, 14–15
Bulgur:
basic Middle Eastern, mix, 123
bulgur in tomato sauce, 124
bulgur with tahini sauce, 124
bulgur with yogurt sauce, 124
Middle Eastern bulgur, 123
quick bulgur casserole, 125
tabule, 125
and chick-pea salad, 99
Burritos, 111
Butter cookies, 195
Butterhorns, whole wheat, 140–41
Buttermilk:
buckwheat pancakes, 15
cornbread, 169
corn griddle cakes, 18
herb dressing, 66
herb soup, 50–51
onion, soup, 39
see also Milk

Cake and cake mixes, 170–92
basic cake mix, 171
apple coffee cake, 177–78
banana-nut cake, 176–77
Boston cream pie, 175–76
carob chip cake, 173
coconut cake, 174–75
frosted orange cake, 173–74
pound cake, 178
sponge cake with carob sauce, 178–79
strawberry shortcake, 179–80
vanilla layer cake with carob frosting, 172
basic carob cake mix, 187
carob cupcakes, 190
carob mint cake, 191–92
carob peanut butter brownies, 191
ice cream roll, 189–90
nutty carob cake, 188–89
sour cream carob cake, 188

basic ginger and spice cake mix, 180
applesauce spice cake, 181
carrot fruit cake, 181–82
English fruit cake, 180–81
frosted carrot cake, 182
fruit and cake dessert, baked, 225–26
gingerbread, 186
peach cake, 183–84
pineapple upside down cake, 187
sour cream spice cake, 183
spice cake, 184–85
yam cake, 185–86
rice flour morning cake, 22
Calcium, 14
Cancer, 4
Caramel:
chip oatmeal bars, 200
-nut muffins, 160–61
Caraway rye bread, 148
Carbohydrates, unrefined, 8
Cardiovascular disorders, 7
Carob:
basic, cake mix, 187
carob cupcakes, 190
carob mint cake, 191–92
carob peanut butter brownies, 191
ice cream roll, 189–90
nutty carob cake, 188–89
sour cream carob cake, 188
basic, pudding mix, 211
carob cake pudding, 213
carob coconut pudding or pie filling, 213
carob cream pie, 211–12
carob ice cream sticks, 214
carob mousse, 215
carob pudding, 211
carob sherbet, 214
rum carob cream pie, 212
chip cake, 173
cookies, 193
caramel chip oatmeal bars, 200
chip, 193
oatmeal, 197–98
frosting:
for carob cupcakes, 190
carob mint cake, 191, 192
sponge cake with, sauce, 178–79
vanilla layer cake with, 172
sauce, sponge cake with, 178–79
Carrot(s):
broth, 53
cake:
frosted, 182
fruit, 181–82
cookies, 204
oatmeal, 199
herb soup, 51
kasha and, 127

Cashew butter:
  nut-, loaf, 158
  rice nut, pancakes, 21
Casseroles:
  bulgur, quick, 125
  curried chick-pea and eggplant, 95
  enchilada, 111
  green pea and millet, 89–90
  kasha, quick, 127
  kidney bean:
    and egg, 108–109
    tomato and onion, baked,
      104–105
  lentil:
    cheese, 101
    crumb, 101
  pinto bean and cheese, 111
  tomato millet, 130
Celery soup, cream of mushroom
  and, 42
Cereals:
  cracked wheat:
    basic malted, mix, 26
    cream, 27–28
    malted, 26
    malted apple, 27
  molasses, wheat germ, raisins
    and nut, 33
  oatmeal:
    apple raisin coconut, 24
    high protein raisin coconut, 23
    raisin coconut oatmeal, 23
  see also Porridge
Challah, whole wheat, 134–35
Cheddar cheese:
  biscuits, 163
  bulgur casserole, quick, 125
  cheesy Spanish rice, 123
  corn bread, 169
  enchilada casserole, 111
  lentil, casserole, 101
  pie crust, 207
  pinto bean and, casserole, 111
  sauce, kidney beans, in, 107–108
  tacos, 110
Cheese:
  blue cheese dressing, 64
  cottage. See Cottage cheese
  cream. See Cream cheese
  cheddar. See Cheddar cheese
  Parmesan. See Parmesan cheese
    mix, basic
  ricotta pie crust, 207
Chemical additives, 7
Chick-pea flour:
  basic light brown mushroom
    soup mix, 43
  light brown mushroom gravy,
    45
  light brown mushroom rice
    soup, 44
  light brown mushroom soup, 43

tomato mushroom cream sauce,
  45
tomato mushroom soup, 44
  vegetable mushroom soup, 44
Chick-pea mix, basic curried, 91
  curried chick-peas, 92
  and eggplant casserole, 95
  with sour cream, 92–93
  stuffed tomatoes, 94
  in tomato sauce, 93–94
Chick-pea mix, basic Middle
  East style, 95
  chick-pea(s):
    and bulgur salad, 99
    humous, 97–98
    Middle East, 95–96
    paté, 97–98
    salad, 98–99
    yogurt stew, 96–97
Chili cornbread, 168
Chowder:
  corn, 37
  potato, 37
  rice, 37
  see also Soups, light, and
    gravy mixes
Christmas drop cookies, 203
Cider jelly muffins, 160
Cinnamon bread, whole wheat
  raisin, 136
Clover leaf rolls, whole wheat, 139–40
Coconut:
  basic coconut crumble or crust
    mix, 208–209
    coconut crumble, 209, 222,
      224, 226
    coconut pie crust, 209
  basic raisin coconut oatmeal
    mix, 23
    apple raisin coconut oatmeal, 24
    fried oatmeal sliced, 24
    high protein raisin coconut
      oatmeal, 23
    oatmeal breakfast bars, 25
    oatmeal French toast, 24–25
    oatmeal morning cookies, 25
  cake, 174–75
  granola, raisin, 32
  pudding or pie filling, 219
  carob, 213
Coffee:
  cake, apple, 177–78
  cream gelatin, 219–20
  pudding, 219
Colds, 8
Commercial mixes compared to
  natural homemade mixes, 5–9
Compote, 223
  jellied, 224
Convenience fast foods, 3, 4
  commercial mixes compared to
    natural homemade mixes, 5–9
Cookies and cookie mixes, 192–204

basic cookie mix, 192
  butter cookies, 195
  carob chip cookies, 193
  carob cookies, 193
  date-filled drop cookies, 194–95
  lemon cookies, 196
  peanut butter cookies, 193–94
  pineapple macaroons, 194
  scones, 196
  vanilla cookies, 192
basic oatmeal cookie mix, 197
  applesauce oatmeal cookies, 199
  caramel chip oatmeal bars, 200
  carob oatmeal cookies, 197–98
  carrot oatmeal cookies, 199
  oatmeal cookies, 197
  oatmeal macaroons, 198
  peanut butter bars, 198–99
basic spice cookie mix, 200–201
  carrot cookies, 204
  Christmas drop cookies, 203
  hermits, 202
  Joe froggers, 201
  rolled spice cookies, 204
  spice crisps, 201
  spice icebox cookies, 203
  spice snaps, 202
morning:
  oatmeal, 25
  wheat, 27
Copper, 14
Corn:
  basic cornbread mix, 167
    buttermilk cornbread, 169
    chili cornbread, 168
    cornbread, 167
    corn cheese bread, 169
    corn muffins, 167–68
    corn-squash muffins, 169
    spoon bread, 168
  basic, wheat griddle cake mix, 17
    breakfast corn raisin muffins, 19
    buttermilk corn griddle cakes, 18
    corn cottage cheese griddle
      cakes, 18
    corn peanut griddle cakes, 19
    corn wheat griddle cakes, 17
  chowder, 37
  cobbler, black-eyed pea and, 78
Cornmeal. See Corn
Cottage cheese:
  corn, griddle cakes, 18
  dill oatmeal bread, 153–54
  dip or sauce, 69
Cracked wheat cereal mix, basic
    malted, 26
  cracked wheat:
    breakfast loaf, 27–28
    cream cereal, 26
    malted, cereal, 26
    malted apple, cereal, 27
    morning, cookies, 27
Cranberry bread, 159

Cream:
  gelatin, coffee, 219–20
  mousse:
    banana, 217–18
    carob, 215
  mushroom, gravy, 43
  mushroom, bisque, 41
  pie(s):
    carob, 211–12
    pineapple, pudding or pie
      filling, 218
    rum carob, 212
    strawberry, 217
    vanilla, 216
  sour cream. See Sour cream
  strawberry shortcake, 179–80
  see also Milk
Cream cheese French dressing, 62
Croquettes, lentil, 101
Cucumber raita, 74
Cupcakes, carob, 190
Curry(ied):
  chick-pea mix. See Chick-pea
    mix, basic curried
  dip, 73
  dressing, 72
    cream, 73
    fruit, 74
    mix, basic, 72
    tomato, 73
  raita, 74
  rice:
    with almonds, 118
    cream, 116
    eggplant, 119
    fruit, 116–17
    tomato, 116
Custard:
  for Boston cream pie, 175, 176
  mincemeat, baked, 222

Dark broth mix, basic, 52
  carrot broth, 53
  dark broth vegetable soup, 54
  dark brown gravy, 54
  dark consommé, 53
  light brown gravy, 54–55
  noodles in dark broth, 53–54
  tomato broth, 53
Dark variety bean mix, basic, 84
  dark variety bean:
    salad, 86–87
    in tomato sauce, 85–86
    and vegetable pot, 85
    and wheat stew, 86
    thick bean stew, 84
Date(s):
  bran, muffins, 166
  carrot fruit cake, 181–82
  -filled drop cookies, 194–95
  nut bread, 157–58
Date sugar, 171
Diabetes, 4, 8

Diet. *See* Nutrition
Dill oatmeal bread, 153–54
Dips:
    cottage cheese, 69
    curry, 73
    garlic tofu, 70
    guacamole, 71
    herb sour cream, 67
    Mexican bean, 112
    Mexican sour cream, 71
    sour cream Parmesan, 60
    yogurt Parmesan, 61
    see also Salad dressings and
        dip mixes
Disease and diet, 4, 7, 8
Dizziness, 7
Doughnuts, yeast whole wheat, 147

Egg(s):
    kidney bean and, casserole,
        108–109
    pastry, 208
    rice ring, 230
Eggplant:
    curried chick-pea and, casserole, 95
    curried rice, 119
    Middle Eastern rice with, 121
Enchilada casserole, 111
English fruit cake, 180–81
English muffins, whole wheat, 141–42
Enriched wheat flour, 8
Equipment, 9–10
European lentil mix. *See* Lentil mix,
        basic European

Facial pressure and MSG, 7
Fast foods, 3, 4
    commercial mixes compared to
        natural homemade mixes, 5–9
Flour, 8
    storing mixes containing, 8
    see also specific types of flour,
        e.g. Brown rice flour; Chick-
        pea flour; Soy bean flour;
        Whole wheat flour; Whole
        wheat pastry flour
French bread, whole wheat, 138
French onion soup, 39
French dressing mix, basic, 61
    beet dressing, 64
    blue cheese dressing, 64
    French dressing, 61
        cream cheese, 62
        fruit, 62
        sour cream, 63
        tomato, 62
    horseradish dressing, 64
    ravigote dressing, 63
French toast, oatmeal, 24–25
Frosting:
    Boston cream pie, 175–76
    carob:
        for carob cupcakes, 190

carob mint cake, 191, 192
    sponge cake with, sauce, 178–79
    vanilla layer cake with, 172
carrot cake, 182
coconut cake, 174–75
nutty carob cake, 189
orange cake, 173–74
peach cake, 184
peanut butter bars, 198, 199
sour cream carob cake, 188
sour cream spice cake, 183
spice cake, 184–85
Fruit:
    basic dried, compote mix, 223
    compote, 223
    dried fruit crisp, 224–25
    dried fruit pie, 224
    dried fruit puree, 225
    fruit and cake dessert, baked,
        226
    jellied compote, 224
    mixed fruit chiffon pie, 226
    Swedish fruit soup, 223
Boston beans with, 82
cake:
    carrot, 181–82
    English, 180–81
curried rice, 116–17
dressing:
    curried, 74
    French, 62
mincemeat. *See* Mincemeat
see also specific fruits

Garam masala, 231
Garlic dressing mix, basic Italian, 67
    cottage cheese dip or sauce, 69
    garlic dressing, 68
        tamari, 68
    garlic sour cream sauce, 69
    garlic tofu dip, 70
    Italian dressing, 68
        creamy, 68
        tomato, 69
Gelatin, coffee cream, 219–20
German puffs, 146
Ginger and spice cake mix, basic, 180
    carrot cake, frosted, 182
    fruit and cake dessert, baked,
        225–26
    fruit cake:
        carrot, 181–82
        English, 180–81
    gingerbread, 186
    peach cake, 183–84
    pineapple upside down cake, 187
    spice cake, 184–85
        applesauce, 181
        sour cream, 183
    yam cake, 185–86
Glazes:
    orange, 143, 144

pecan, 145
yam cake, 185, 186
Grains and grain mixes. *See specific
  grains, e.g.* Buckwheat; Kasha;
  Oats
Granola, 14
  coconut raisin, 32
  sesame buckwheat, 31–32
  variety flake, 31
Gravy mixes. *See* Soups, light, and
  gravy mixes
Green peas. *See* Split green pea
  mix, basic
Griddle cakes:
  buttermilk corn, 18
  corn cottage cheese, 18
  corn peanut butter, 19
  corn wheat, 17–18
  mix, basic corn wheat, 17
Grocery shopping, 10–11
Guacamole, 71

Hamburger Helper, 7–8
Heart ailments, 7
Herb 'n onion millet mix, basic, 128
  millet:
    herb onion, 128–29
    patties, 129
    in tahini sauce, 129
    tomato, 130
    tomato, casserole, 130
Herb broth mix, basic, 50
  buttermilk herb soup, 50–51
  carrot herb soup, 51
  herb broth, 50
  herb noodle soup, 51
  herb sauce, 52
  herb vegetable soup, 51
  non-dairy herb cream soup, 52
  tomato herb soup, 50
Herb dressing mix, basic, 65
  herb dressing, 65
    buttermilk, 66
    cream, 65
    tahini, 67
    tomato, 66
    tomato cream, 66
  herb sour cream dip, 67
Hermits, 202
High blood pressure, 7
Hiziki seaweed, 231
  see also Seaweed soup mix,
    basic Japanese
Honey, 170–71
Horseradish dressing, 64
Humous, 97–98
Hypertension, 7
Hypoglycemia, 8

Icebox cookies, spice, 203
Ice cream:
  roll, 189–90

sticks, carob, 214
Indian rice pilaf mix, basic, 115
  curried rice:
    with almonds, 118
    cream, 116
    eggplant, 119
    fruit, 116–17
    tomato, 116
  Indian rice pilaf, 115
  lentil rice pilaf, 118
  mushroom pilaf, 117
  peas pilaf, 117
  yellow pea rice pilaf, 118
Inflation, 3, 4
Inositol, 14
Iron, 14
Italian dressing, 70
  creamy, 68
  mix, basic Italian garlic, 67

Japanese seaweed soup mix, basic, 47
  Japanese seaweed soup, 48
  seaweed noodle soup, 49
  seaweed rice soup, 48
  seaweed sauce, 49
  seaweed sesame rice soup, 48
  seaweed tofu soup, 49
Jars and bottles, 9–10
Jellied compote, 224
Jellied mincemeat, 221–22
Jellied rice, 230
Jell-O, 8
Jelly muffins, cider, 160
Joe froggers, 201

Kasha (buckwheat groats):
  basic spiced, mix, 125–26
    buckwheat patties, 126–27
    kasha and carrots, 127
    kasha in tomato sauce, 128
    kasha in yogurt, 127–28
    kasha loaf, 126
    quick kasha casserole, 127
    spiced kasha, 126
  granola, sesame, 31–32
Kidney bean mix, basic, 103
  kidney bean(s):
    in cheese sauce, 107–108
    dinner salad, 104
    and egg casserole, 108–109
    in sour cream with whole
      potatoes, 106–107
    stew, 103–104
    stuffed pumpkin, 105
    tomato and onion casserole,
      baked, 104–105
    in tomato sauce, 105–106
Kidney disorders, 7

Labels, 10
Lemon cookies, 196

Lentil(s):
 basic European, mix, 99
 lentil cheese casserole, 101
 lentil croquettes, 101
 lentil crumb casserole, 101
 lentil loaf, 100
 lentil pot pie, 102
 lentil salad, 102
 lentil Shepherd's pie, 102–103
 lentil stew, 100
 rice pilaf, 118

Macaroons:
 oatmeal, 198
 pineapple, 194
Magnesium, 14
Malt. See Barley malt
Maple sugar, granulated, 171
Mexican dressing or sauce mix,
  basic spicy, 70
 creamy Mexican salad dressing, 72
 guacamole, 71
 Mexican sour cream dip, 71
 spicy Mexican dressing, 70
 taco sauce, 71
Mexican pinto bean mix, basic, 109
 burritos, 111
 enchilada casserole, 111
 Mexican bean dip, 112
 Mexican pinto beans, 109–10
 Mexican stew, 112–13
 pinto bean and cheese casserole,
  111
 refried beans, 112
 tacos, 110
Middle East style:
 bulgur mix. See Bulgur, basic
  Middle Eastern, mix
 chick-pea mix. See Chick-pea mix,
  basic Middle East style
 rice pilaf mix. See Rice, basic
  Middle Eastern, pilaf mix
Milk:
 ABC soup, cream of, 46
 basic cream of mushroom soup
  mix, 41
  cream of mushroom and celery
   soup, 42
  cream of mushroom soup, 41
  mushroom bisque, 41
  mushroom cream gravy, 43
  mushroom rice soup, 42
  pumpkin mushroom soup or
   sauce, 42
 basic cream of onion soup mix, 36
  corn chowder, 37
  cream of onion soup, 36
  onion cream sauce, 38
  potato chowder, 37
  rice chowder, 37
  tomato onion cream soup, 36
 custard:
  for Boston cream pie, 175, 176

 mincemeat, baked, 222
 mousse:
  banana, 217–18
  carob, 215
 puddings. See Pudding
 rice ring, 230
 sweet cream soup, 56
 vanilla sticks, frozen, 218
 whole wheat, bread, 133–34
 see also Buttermilk; Cream
Millet:
 basic herb 'n onion, mix, 128
  herb onion millet, 128–29
  millet in tahini sauce, 129
  millet patties, 129
  tomato millet, 130
  tomato millet casserole, 130
 basic spiced, porridge mix, 28
  apple millet porridge, 29
  creamed millet porridge, 29
  milky millet porridge, 29
  millet breakfast patties, 30
  spiced millet porridge, 28
 green pea and, casserole, 89–90
Mincemeat mix, basic, 220
 baked mincemeat custard, 222
 jellied mincemeat, 221–22
 mincemeat, 220
 mincemeat crumble, 222
 mincemeat pie, 221
 mincemeat tahini pudding, 221
Minerals, 6
Mint cake, carob, 191–92
Miso paste, 231
 basic clear onion soup mix, 38
  brown onion gravy, 40
  clear onion soup, 38
  French onion soup, 39
  onion buttermilk soup, 39
  onion tomato soup, 39
  onion vegetable soup, 40
  pureed onion vegetable soup, 40
 basic dark broth mix, 52
  carrot broth, 53
  dark broth vegetable soup, 54
  dark brown gravy, 54
  dark consommé, 53
  light brown gravy, 54–55
  noodles in dark broth, 53–54
  tomato broth, 53
 basic light brown mushroom soup
  mix, 43
  light brown mushroom gravy, 45
  light brown mushroom rice soup,
   44
  light brown mushroom soup, 43
  tomato mushroom cream sauce,
   45
  tomato mushroom soup, 44
  vegetable mushroom soup, 44
 seaweed soup mix, basic Japanese,
  47

Japanese seaweed soup, 48
seaweed noodle soup, 49
seaweed rice soup, 48
seaweed sauce, 49
seaweed sesame rice soup, 48
seaweed tofu soup, 49
Molasses. *See* Blackstrap molasses
Monosodium glutamate, 7
Morning cake, rice flour, 22
Morning cookies:
oatmeal, 25
wheat, 27
Mousse:
banana, 217–18
carob, 215
MSG, 7
Muffin(s):
apple, 161–62
basic bran, mix, 164
apple-bran muffins, 165
banana-bran muffins, 165–66
bran date muffins, 166
bran muffins, 164
pumpkin-bran muffins, 166
yogurt-bran muffins, 165
basic quick whole wheat bread or,
mix. *See* Whole wheat flour,
basic quick whole wheat bread
or muffin mix
blueberry, 161
breakfast corn raisin, 19
caramel-nut, 160–61
cider jelly, 160
corn, 167–68
-squash, 169
English, whole wheat, 141–42
German puffs, 146
oatmeal, 155
pineapple, 160
simple, 159
see also Rolls
Mushroom(s):
basic cream of, soup mix, 41
cream of mushroom and celery
soup, 42
cream of mushroom soup, 41
mushroom bisque, 41
mushroom cream gravy, 43
mushroom rice soup, 42
pumpkin mushroom soup or
sauce, 42
basic light brown mushroom soup
mix, 43
light brown mushroom gravy, 45
light brown mushroom rice
soup, 44
light brown mushroom soup, 43
tomato mushroom cream sauce,
45
tomato mushroom soup, 44
vegetable mushroom soup, 44
pilaf, 117

Natural homemade mixes:
basic information about, 4–5, 9–12
commercial mixes compared to, 5–9
for chemical additives and
flavorings, 7
for cost, 9
for nutritional vlaue, 5–6
for sugar content, 7–8
for unrefined carbohydrates, 8
equipment, 9–10
refilling the empties, 12
shopping for ingredients, 10–11
storage of, 10, 11, 35
technique for making, 11
using, advice on, 11–12
versatility of each mix, 12
Noodle(s):
in dark broth, 53–54
date-filled drop cookies, 194–95
soup
herb, 51
seaweed, 49
Nutrition, 3–4, 10
comparison of natural and
commercial mixes, 5–8
Nuts:
basic, and raisin soup mix, 55
nutty sweet and sour sauce, 57
nutty tomato soup, 56
sweet and sour rice soup, 56
sweet and sour soup, 55
sweet and sour tomato sauce, 57
sweet cream soup, 56
basic coconut crumble or crust
mix, 208–209
coconut crumble, 209, 222, 224,
226
coconut pie crust, 209
basic sweet and nutty rice dessert
mix, 226
apple nut rice dessert, 228
baked rice dessert, 228–29
fluffy rice pudding, 229
hearty rice pudding, 227
jellied rice, 230
orange sweet rice dessert, 227
peach 'n nutty rice dessert, 228
pineapple rice pudding, 229
rice ring, 230
sweet rice dessert, 227
basic wheat germ crumble mix, 210
wheat germ crumble, 210,
222, 224
wheat germ pie crust, 210, 226
bread:
-butter loaf, 158
cranberry, 159
date-, 157–58
orange-, loaf, 158–59
cake, banana-, 176–77
caramel chip oatmeal bars, 200
molasses, wheat germ, raisins
and, cereal, 33

Nuts (*continued*)
  muffins, caramel-, 160–61
  nutty carob cake, 188–89
  pecan rolls, 145–46
  see also specific types of nuts

Oatmeal. *See* Oats
Oats:
  basic coconut crumble or crust
    mix, 208–209
    coconut crumble, 209, 222, 224
    coconut pie crust, 209
  basic oatmeal cookie mix, 197
    applesauce oatmeal cookies, 199
    caramel chip oatmeal bars, 200
    carob oatmeal cookies, 197–98
    carrot oatmeal cookies, 199
    oatmeal cookies, 197
    oatmeal macaroons, 198
    peanut butter bars, 198–99
  basic oatmeal wheat bread mix, 152
    dill oatmeal bread, 153–54
    oatmeal batter bread, 153
    oatmeal bread, 153
    oatmeal muffins, 155
    raisin oatmeal bread, 154
  basic raisin coconut oatmeal mix,
    23
    apple raisin coconut oatmeal, 24
    fried oatmeal slices, 24
    high protein raisin coconut
      oatmeal, 23
    oatmeal breakfast bars, 25
    oatmeal French toast, 24–25
    oatmeal morning cookies, 25
    raisin coconut oatmeal cereal, 23
  granola:
    coconut raisin, 32
    sesame buckwheat, 31–32
    variety flake, 31
Obesity, 8
Onion(s):
  basic clear, soup mix, 38
    brown onion gravy, 40
    clear onion soup, 38
    French onion soup, 39
    onion buttermilk soup, 39
    onion tomato soup, 39
    onion vegetable soup, 40
    pureed onion vegetable soup, 40
  basic cream of, soup mix, 36
    corn chowder, 37
    cream of onion soup, 36
    onion cream sauce, 38
    potato chowder, 37
    rice chowder, 37
    tomato onion cream soup, 36
  basic herb 'n, millet mix, 128
    herb onion millet, 128–29
    millet in tahini sauce, 129
    millet patties, 129
    tomato millet, 130
    tomato millet casserole, 130

bread, whole wheat, 137
kidney bean and tomato casserole,
    baked, 104–105
Orange:
  biscuits, 162
  cake, frosted, 173–74
  glazed rolls, 143–44
    orange butter for, 143
    orange glaze for, 144
  sweet rice dessert, 227

Pancakes:
  buckwheat, 15
    apple, 16
    applesauce and sour cream, 16
    blueberry, 17
  buttermilk, 15
  mix, basic, 14–15
  rice flour, 20
  rice molasses, 20
  rice nut butter, 21
Pantothenic acid, 14
Parmesan cheese mix, basic, 59
  Parmesan soy dressing, 60
  sour cream Parmesan dip, 60
  sweet and sour Parmesan cheese
    dressing, 60
  tomato cheese salad dressing, 59
  vinegar cheese dressing, 59
  yogurt Parmesan dip, 61
Paté:
  humous, 97–98
  Middle Eastern chick-pea, 97–98
Peach:
  cake, 183–84
  'n nutty rice dessert, 228
Peanut butter:
  bars, 198–99
  brownies, carob, 191
  cookies, 193–94
  corn, griddle cakes, 19
  nut-butter loaf, 158
  rice nut, pancakes, 21
Peas:
  black-eyed. *See* Black-eyed pea
    mix, basic Southern
  pilaf, 117
  split green pea. *See* Split green
    pea mix, basic
  split yellow, rice pilaf, 118
Pecan(s):
  banana-nut cake, 176–77
  caramel chip oatmeal bars, 200
  caramel-nut muffins, 160–61
  date-filled drop cookies, 194–95
  date-nut bread, 157–58
  nutty carob cake, 188–89
  rolls, 145–46
Peppers, black-eyed pea stuffed, 78
Phosphorus, 8, 14
Pies and pie mixes, 205–10
  banana pudding or, filling, 216–17

basic coconut crumble or crust
  mix, 208–209
  coconut crumble, 209, 222, 224,
    226
  coconut pie crust, 209
basic wheat germ crumble mix, 210
  wheat germ crumble, 210, 222,
    224
  wheat germ pie crust, 210, 226
basic whole wheat pie crust mix,
  205
  cheddar cheese pie crust, 207
  egg pastry, 208
  ricotta pie crust, 207
  rolled pie crust, 206
  sour cream pie crust, 207–208
  whole wheat crumble topping,
    206, 222, 224
black-eyed pea, 77–78
carob coconut pudding or, filling,
  213
carob cream, 211–12
  rum, 212
fruit:
  dried, 224
  mixed, chiffon, 226
lentil:
  pot, 102
  Shepherd's, 102–103
mincemeat, 221
pineapple pudding or, filling, 219
strawberry cream, 217
vanilla cream, 216
Pineapple:
  cream pudding or pie filling, 218
  macaroons, 194
  muffins, 160
  rice pudding, 229
  upside down cake, 187
Pinto bean mix, basic Mexican, 109
  burritos, 111
  enchilada casserole, 111
  Mexican bean dip, 112
  Mexican pinto beans, 109–10
  Mexican stew, 112–13
  pinto bean and cheese casserole,
    111
  refried beans, 112
  tacos, 110
Pizza dough, 139
Porridge, millet:
  apple, 29
  basic spiced, mix, 28
  breakfast patties, 30
  creamed, 29
  milky, 29
  spiced, 28
Potassium, 8, 14
Potato(es):
  chowder, 37
  kidney beans in sour cream
    sauce with, 106–107
Pound cake, 178

Preservatives, 7
Pretzels, soft whole wheat, 144
Protein, 5–6
Pudding:
  basic, mix, 215
  banana mousse, 217–18
  banana pudding or pie filling,
    216–17
  coconut pudding or pie filling,
    219
  coffee cream gelatin, 219–20
  coffee pudding, 219
  pineapple cream pudding or
    pie filling, 218
  strawberry cream pie, 217
  vanilla cream pie, 216
  vanilla pudding, 215–16
  vanilla sticks, frozen, 218
  basic carob, mix, 211
  carob cake pudding, 213
  carob coconut pudding or pie
    filling, 213
  carob cream pie, 211–12
  carob ice cream sticks, 214
  carob mousse, 215
  carob pudding, 211
  carob sherbet, 214
  rum carob cream pie, 212
mincemeat tahini, 221
rice:
  fluffy, 229
  hearty, 227
  pineapple, 229
Puffed Wheat:
  malted wheat cakes, 32–33
  sweet wheat puffs, 33–34
Pumpernickel bread, old time, 150–51
Pumpkin:
  bread, 157
  kidney bean stuffed, 105
  mushroom soup or sauce, 42

Raisin(s):
  basic, coconut oatmeal mix, 23
  apple raisin coconut oatmeal, 24
  fried oatmeal slices, 24
  high protein raisin coconut
    oatmeal, 23
  oatmeal breakfast bars, 25
  oatmeal French toast, 24–25
  oatmeal morning cookies, 25
  basic nut and, soup mix, 55
  nutty sweet and sour sauce, 57
  nutty tomato soup, 56
  sweet and sour rice soup, 56
  sweet and sour soup, 56
  sweet and sour tomato sauce, 57
  sweet cream soup, 56
bread:
  oatmeal, 154
  whole wheat, cinnamon, 136
  whole wheat loaf, quick, 156
granola, coconut, 32

Raisin(s) (*continued*)
  molasses, wheat germ and nut
    cereal, 33
  muffins, breakfast corn, 19
Raita, 74
Ravigote dressing, 63
Recommended Daily Allowance
  (RDA), 5–6, 7
Refried beans, 112
Rice, 114–23
  basic Indian, pilaf mix, 115
    cream curried rice, 116
    curried rice with almonds, 118
    eggplant curried rice, 119
    fruit curried rice, 116–17
    Indian rice pilaf, 115
    lentil rice pilaf, 118
    mushroom pilaf, 117
    peas pilaf, 117
    tomato rice curry, 116
    yellow pea rice pilaf, 118
  basic Middle Eastern, pilaf mix, 119
    Middle Eastern flavored rice, 119
    Middle Eastern rice in tomato
      sauce, 120–21
    Middle Eastern rice in tahini
      sauce, 120
    Middle Eastern rice with
      eggplant, 121
    sesame rice yogurt, 120
  basic Spanish, mix, 121
    cheesy Spanish rice, 123
    creamy Spanish rice, 122
    Spanish rice, 122
    spicy rice, 122
  basic sweet and nutty, dessert
    mix, 226
    apple nut rice dessert, 228
    baked rice dessert, 228–29
    fluffy rice pudding, 229
    hearty rice pudding, 227
    jellied rice, 230
    orange sweet rice dessert, 227
    peach 'n nutty rice dessert, 228
    pineapple rice pudding, 229
    rice ring, 230
    sweet rice dessert, 227
  chowder, 37
  and green pea stew, 88–89
  soup:
    light brown mushroom, 44
    mushroom, 42
    seaweed, 48
    seaweed sesame, 48
    sweet and sour, 56
Rice flour. *See* Brown rice flour
Ricotta cheese pie crust, 207
Rolled pie crust, 206
Rolled spice cookies, 204
Rolls:
  whole wheat:
    butterhorns, 140–41
    clover leaf, 139–40

orange glazed, 143–44
pecan, 145–46
see also Muffins
Rum carob cream pie, 212
Rye flakes, variety flake granola, 31
Rye flour:
  basic rye bread mix, 147–48
  caraway rye bread, 148
  old time pumpernickel bread,
    150–51
  rye bread sticks, 151
  Swedish rye bread, 149–50
  Swiss rye bread, 149

Salad(s):
  chick-pea, 98–99
    and bulgur, 99
  dark variety bean, 86–87
  kidney bean dinner, 104
  lentil, 102
Salad dressings and dip mixes, 58–74
  curried dressing mix, basic, 72
  French dressing mix, basic, 61
  herb dressing mix, basic, 65
  Italian garlic dressing mix, basic, 67
  Mexican dressing or sauce mix,
    basic spicy, 70
  Parmesan cheese mix, basic, 59
  see also specific mixes
Salt in commercial mixes, 7
Sara Lee cake, 8
Sauce(s):
  carob, sponge cake with, 178–79
  Cheddar cheese, kidney beans in,
    107–108
  cottage cheese, 69
  herb, 52
  Mexican dressing or, mix, basic
    spicy, 70
  onion cream, 38
  seaweed, 49
  sour cream:
    garlic, 69
    kidney beans in, with whole
      potatoes, 106–107
  sweet and sour:
    nutty, 57
    tomato, 57
  tahini:
    bulgur with, 124
    Middle Eastern rice with, 120
    millet in, 129
  tomato:
    bulgur in, 124
    curried chick-peas in, 93
    kasha in, 128
    kidney beans in, 105–106
    Middle Eastern rice in, 120–21
    sweet and sour, 57
  yogurt, bulgur with, 124
Scones, 196
Seaweed soup mix, basic Japanese, 47

seaweed soup:
Japanese, 48
noodle, 49
rice, 48
sesame rice, 48
tofu, 49
seaweed sauce, 49
Sesame (seeds):
buckwheat granola, 31–32
rice yogurt, 120
Shepherd's pie, lentil, 102–103
Sherbet, carob, 214
Shopping, 10–11
Shortcake, strawberry, 179–80
Simple muffins, 159
Skin disorders, 7
Soba, 231
seaweed noodle soup, 49
Soups, light, and gravy mixes, 35–57
ABC soup mix, basic, 45
dark broth mix, basic, 52
herb broth mix, basic, 50
mushroom soup mix:
basic cream of, 41
basic light brown, 43
nut and raisin soup mix, basic, 55
onion soup mix:
basic clear, 38
basic cream of, 36
seaweed soup mix, basic Japanese, 47
see also specific mixes
Sour cream:
and applesauce buckwheat cakes, 16
carob cake, 188
creamy Spanish rice, 122
curried chick-peas with, 92–93
curried rice, 116
curry cream dressing, 73
curry dip, 73
French dressing, 63
herb:
cream dressing, 65
dip, 67
tomato cream dressing, 66
Mexican, dip, 71
Mexican salad dressing, creamy, 72
Parmesan dip, 60
pie crust, 207–208
sauce:
garlic, 69
kidney beans in, with whole potatoes, 106–107
spice cake, 183
Southern black-eyed pea mix. *See* Black-eyed pea mix, basic Southern
Southern hopping John, 76–77
Soybean flour:
basic light brown mushroom soup mix, 43
light brown mushroom gravy, 45

light brown mushroom rice soup, 44
light brown mushroom soup, 43
tomato mushroom cream sauce, 45
tomato mushroom soup, 44
vegetable mushroom soup, 44
Soy sauce. *See* Tamari soy sauce
Spice and ginger cake mix, basic, 180
carrot cake, frosted, 182
fruit and cake dessert, baked, 225–26
fruit cake:
carrot, 181–82
English, 180–81
gingerbread, 186
peach cake, 183–84
pineapple upside down cake, 187
spice cake, 184–85
applesauce, 181
sour cream, 183
yam cake, 185–86
Spice cookie mix, basic, 200–201
carrot cookies, 204
Christmas drop cookies, 203
hermits, 202
Joe froggers, 201
rolled spice cookies, 204
spice crisps, 201
spice icebox cookies, 203
spice snaps, 202
Split green pea mix, basic, 87
green pea:
and millet casserole, 89–90
and rice stew, 88–89
soup, hearty, 88
and vegetable soup, 90–91
Split yellow pea rice pilaf, 118
Spoon bread, 168
Squash:
acorn. *See* Acorn squash
corn-, muffins, 169
Stew:
bean:
dark variety, and wheat, 86
kidney, 103–104
lentil, 100
sweet and sour, 83
thick, 84
green pea and rice, 88–89
Mexican, 112–13
Storage of mixes, 10, 11
Strawberry:
cream pie, 217
jellied rice, 230
shortcake, 179–80
Sugar, 170, 171
in commercial mixes, 7–8
see also Sweeteners
Swedish fruit soup, 223
Swedish rye bread, 149–50
Sweet and nutty rice dessert mix. *See* Rice, basic sweet and nutty, dessert mix

Sweet and sour:
  bean stew, 83
  salad dressing, Parmesan cheese,
    60
  soup, 55
  rice, 56
Sweeteners, 14, 170–71
  see also Sugar
Swiss rye bread, 149

Tabule, 125
Tacos, 110
Taco sauce, 71
Tahini, 231
  herb, dressing, 67
  humous, 97–98
  Middle Eastern chick-pea paté,
    97–98
  millet breakfast patties, 30
  mincemeat, pudding, 221
  sauce:
    bulgur with, 124
    Middle Eastern rice in, 120
    millet in, 129
  seaweed sesame rice soup, 48
Tamari soy sauce:
  broth ABC soup, 46
  garlic dressing, 68
  Parmesan dressing, 60
Thick bean stew, 84
Tofu:
  dip, garlic, 70
  seaweed, soup, 49
Tomato(es):
  black-eyed pea and, dinner, 79
  chick-pea stuffed, 94
  kidney bean and onion casserole,
    baked, 104–105
  millet, 130
    casserole, 130
  rice curry, 116
  salad dressing:
    cheese, 59
    curried, 72
    French, 62
    herb, 66
    Italian, 69
    tomato cream, 66
  sauce:
    beans in, 85–86
    bulgur in, 124
    curried chick-peas in, 93–94
    kidney beans in, 105–106
    Middle Eastern rice in, 120–21
    mushroom cream, 45
    kasha in, 128
    sweet and sour, 57
  soup:
    broth, 53
    herb, 50
    onion, 39
    onion cream, 37
    mushroom, 44

  nutty, 56
Tooth decay, 8, 171
Tortillas:
  burritos, 111
  enchilada casserole, 111
Turnovers, Boston bean, 81

U.S. Senate Select Committee on
  Human Needs and Nutrition,
  3, 7

Vanilla:
  cookies, 192
  cream pie, 216
  layer cake with carob frosting, 172
  pudding, 215–16
  sticks, frozen, 218
Vegetable(s):
  Mexican stew, 112–13
  pot, variety bean and, 85
  soup:
    dark broth, 54
    green pea and, 90–91
    herb, 51
    mushroom, 44
    onion, 40
    pureed onion, 40
  see also specific vegetables
Vinegar cheese dressing, 59
Vitamin B-complex, 8, 14
Vitamin E, 14
Vitamins, 5–6

Walnuts:
  banana-nut cake, 176–77
  caramel chip oatmeal bars, 200
  caramel-nut muffins, 160–61
  cranberry bread, 159
  date-filled drop cookies, 194–95
  date-nut bread, 157–58
  nutty carob cake, 188–89
  orange-nut loaf, 158–59
Wheat berries, dark variety bean
  and, stew, 86
Wheat flakes, variety flake granola, 31
Wheat germ:
  basic, crumble mix, 210
    wheat germ crumble, 210, 222,
      224
    wheat germ pie crust, 210, 226
  basic coconut crumble or crust
    mix, 208–209
    coconut crumble, 209, 222, 224,
      226
    coconut pie crust, 209
  basic cookie mix, 192
    butter cookies, 195
    carob chip cookies, 193
    carob cookies, 193
    date-filled drop cookies, 194–95
    lemon cookies, 196
    peanut butter cookies, 193–94
    pineapple macaroons, 194

scones, 196
vanilla cookies, 192
granola:
  coconut raisin, 32
  variety flake, 31
molasses, raisins and nut cereal, 33
Wheat puffs. *See* Puffed Wheat
Whey, Swiss rye bread, 149
Whole grain flours and pastas, 8,
  35, 114
  *see also specific types of whole
    grain flours and pastas*
Whole wheat ABC pasta:
  basic ABC soup mix, 45
  ABC bean soup, 47
  ABC soup, 46
  cream of ABC soup, 46
  non-dairy ABC soup, 47
  tamari broth ABC soup, 46
Whole wheat flour:
  basic all-purpose whole wheat bread
    mix, 132
  German puffs, 146
  orange glazed rolls, 143–44
  pizza dough, 139
  soft whole wheat pretzels, 144
  whole wheat bagels, 142
  whole wheat bread, 132–33
  whole wheat butterhorns, 140–41
  whole wheat challah, 134–35
  whole wheat clover leaf rolls,
    139–40
  whole wheat French bread, 138
  whole wheat milk bread, 133–34
  whole wheat onion bread, 137
  whole wheat quick bread, 135
  whole wheat raisin cinnamon
    bread, 136
  yeast whole wheat doughnuts,
    147
basic bran muffin mix, 164
  apple-bran muffins, 165
  banana-bran muffins, 165–66
  bran date muffins, 166
  bran muffins, 164
  pumpkin-bran muffins, 166
  yogurt-bran muffins, 165
basic coconut crumble or crust
  mix, 208–209
  coconut crumble, 209, 222, 224,
    226
  coconut pie crust, 209
basic cornbread mix, 167
  buttermilk cornbread, 169
  chili cornbread, 168
  cornbread, 167
  corn cheese bread, 169
  corn muffins, 167–68
  corn-squash muffins, 169
  spoon bread, 168
basic oatmeal wheat bread mix, 152
  dill oatmeal bread, 153–54
  oatmeal bread, 153

oatmeal butter bread, 153
oatmeal muffins, 155
raisin oatmeal bread, 154
basic quick whole wheat bread or
  muffin mix, 155
  apple muffins, 161–62
  banana bread, 156–57
  blueberry muffins, 161
  caramel nut muffins, 160–61
  cheese biscuits, 163
  cider jelly muffins, 160
  cranberry bread, 159
  date-nut bread, 157–58
  nut-butter loaf, 158
  orange biscuits, 162
  orange-nut loaf, 158–59
  pineapple muffins, 160
  pumpkin bread, 157
  quick whole wheat loaf, 156
  quick whole wheat raisin loaf,
    156
  rolled biscuits, 163–64
  simple muffins, 159
  whole wheat drop muffins, 162
  yogurt biscuits, 163
basic rye bread mix, 147–48
  caraway rye bread, 148
  old time pumpernickel bread,
    150–51
  rye bread sticks, 151
  Swedish rye bread, 149–50
  Swiss rye bread, 149
basic wheat germ pie crumble mix,
  210
  wheat germ crumble, 210, 222,
    224
  wheat germ pie crust, 210, 226
Whole wheat pastry flour:
  basic buckwheat pancake mix,
    14–15
  apple buckwheat pancakes, 16
  applesauce and sour cream
    buckwheat cakes, 16
  buckwheat blueberry pancakes,
    17
  buckwheat pancakes, 15
  buttermilk buckwheat pancakes,
    15
basic cake mix, 171
  apple coffee cake, 177–78
  banana-nut cake, 176–77
  Boston cream pie, 175–76
  carob chip cake, 173
  coconut cake, 174–75
  frosted orange cake, 173–74
  pound cake, 178
  sponge cake with carob sauce,
    178–79
  strawberry shortcake, 179–80
  vanilla layer cake with carob
    frosting, 172
basic carob cake mix, 187
  carob cupcakes, 190

Whole wheat pastry flour
(*continued*)
    carob mint cake, 191–92
    carob peanut butter brownies,
      191
    ice cream roll, 189–90
    nutty carob cake, 188–89
    sour cream carob cake, 188
    basic cookie mix, 192
      butter cookies, 195
      carob chip cookies, 193
      carob cookies, 193
      date-filled drop cookies, 194–95
      lemon cookies, 196
      peanut butter cookies, 193–94
      pineapple macaroons, 194
      scones, 196
      vanilla cookies, 192
    basic corn wheat griddle cake mix,
      17
      breakfast corn raisin muffins, 19
      buttermilk corn griddle cakes, 18
      corn cottage cheese griddle
        cakes, 18
      corn peanut butter griddle cakes,
        19
      corn wheat griddle cakes, 17–18
    basic cream of onion soup mix, 36
      cream of onion soup, 36
      corn chowder, 37
      onion cream sauce, 38
      potato chowder, 37
      rice chowder, 37
      tomato onion cream soup, 36
    basic cream of mushroom soup
      mix, 41
      cream of mushroom and celery
        soup, 42
      cream of mushroom soup, 41
      mushroom bisque, 41
      mushroom cream gravy, 43
      mushroom rice soup, 42
      pumpkin mushroom soup or
        sauce, 42
    basic ginger and spice cake mix,
      180
      applesauce spice cake, 181
      carrot fruit cake, 181–82
      English fruit cake, 180–81
      frosted carrot cake, 182
      gingerbread, 186
      peach cake, 183–84
      pineapple upside down cake, 187
      sour cream spice cake, 183
      spice cake, 184–85
      yam cake, 185–86
    basic oatmeal cookie mix, 197
      applesauce oatmeal cookies, 199
      caramel chip oatmeal bars, 200
      carob oatmeal cookies, 197–98
      carrot oatmeal cookies, 199
      oatmeal cookies, 197
      oatmeal macaroons, 198

    peanut butter bars, 198–99
basic quick whole wheat bread or
    muffin mix, 155
    apple muffins, 161–62
    banana bread, 156–57
    blueberry muffins, 161
    caramel nut muffins, 160–61
    cheese biscuits, 163
    cider jelly muffins, 160
    cranberry bread, 159
    date-nut bread, 157–58
    nut-butter bread, 158
    orange biscuits, 162
    orange-nut loaf, 158–59
    pineapple muffins, 160
    pumpkin bread, 157
    quick whole wheat loaf, 156
    quick whole wheat raisin loaf,
      156
    rolled biscuits, 163–64
    simple muffins, 159
    whole wheat drop muffins, 162
    yogurt biscuits, 163
basic rice griddle cake mix, 19–20
    rice apple griddle cakes, 21
    rice flour morning cake, 22
    rice flour pancakes, 20
    rice molasses pancakes, 20
    rice nut butter pancakes, 21
basic spice cookie mix, 200–201
    carrot cookies, 204
    Christmas drop cookies, 203
    hermits, 202
    Joe froggers, 201
    rolled spice cookies, 204
    spice crisps, 201
    spice icebox cookies, 203
    spice snaps, 202
basic whole wheat pie crust mix,
    205
    cheddar cheese pie crust, 207
    egg pastry, 208
    ricotta pie crust, 207
    rolled pie crust, 206
    sour cream pie crust, 207–208
    whole wheat crumble topping,
      206, 222, 224
non-dairy herb cream sauce, 52
Winter squash-corn muffins, 169
Wyler's Beef Bouillon, 7

Yam cake, 185–86
Yeast mixes. *See* Bread and yeast
    mixes, quick
Yogurt:
    biscuits, 163
    -bran muffins, 165
    kasha in, 127–28
    Parmesan dip, 61
    raita, 74
    sauce, bulgur with, 124
    sesame rice, 120